JACKSON'S POI

ONTARIO'S FIRST COTTAGE COU RY

The Black River at Jackson's Point around 1910.

– METROPOLITAN TORONTO REFERENCE LIBRARY POSTCARD COLLECTION

JACKSON'S POINT
ONTARIO'S FIRST COTTAGE COUNTRY

Stoddart

❦ JEANNE HOPKINS ❦
A BOSTON MILLS PRESS BOOK

Canadian Cataloguing in Publication Data

Hopkins, Jeanne 1939-

JACKSON'S POINT: Ontario's first cottage country

Includes bibliographical references.
ISBN 1-55046-053-6

1. Jackson's Point (Ont.) – History.
2. Jackson's Point (Ont.) – Biography.   I. Title.

FC3095.J32H66   1993   917.3'547   C93-093617-5
F1059.J32H66   1993

Printed in Canada

First published in 1993 by
Stoddart Publishing Co. Limited
34 Lesmill Road
Toronto, Canada M3B 2T6
(416) 445-3333

A BOSTON MILLS PRESS BOOK
The Boston Mills Press
132 Main Street
Erin, Ontario N0B 1T0

The publisher gratefully acknowledges the support of the
Canada Council, Ontario Ministry of Culture and Communications,
Ontario Arts Council and Ontario Publishing Centre
in the development of writing and publishing in Canada.

FRONT COVER

*Enjoying the pure, clear waters on the shores of
Lake Simcoe at Springwood around the turn of the century.*

– GEORGINA HISTORICAL SOCIETY POSTCARD COLLECTION

BACK COVER

Travellers boarding the ferry Islay *at Jackson's Point
on a bright summer day in 1911.*

– CITY OF TORONTO ARCHIVES   SC 244-2409

PRECEDING PAGES

*Jackson's Point was a popular picnic spot and
cottage resort for Torontonians in the 1890s.*

– METROPOLITAN TORONTO REFERENCE LIBRARY, FROM *HIGHLANDS
OF ONTARIO BY THE GRAND TRUNK RAILWAY SYSTEM*

Enjoying a picnic at Jackson's Point in the early 1900s.

– METROPOLITAN TORONTO REFERENCE LIBRARY POSTCARD COLLECTION

TABLE OF CONTENTS

ACKNOWLEDGMENTS   7

ONTARIO'S FIRST COTTAGE COUNTRY   9

EARLY SETTLERS AND THEIR FAMILIES   12

    JOHN MILLS JACKSON   12

    WILLIAM BOURCHIER   14

    JAMES O'BRIEN BOURCHIER   15

    WILLIAM JOHNSON   16

    JOHN COMER   17

    THOMAS MOSSINGTON   18

    SIMON LEE   19

    WILLIAM KINGDOM RAINS   20

    SUSAN SIBBALD   22

ST. GEORGE'S ANGLICAN CHURCH   25

ST. GEORGE'S CEMETERY   27

LANDMARKS   32

    THE BRIARS   32

    THE BRIARS GOLF CLUB   34

    SPRING HOUSE   35

    GLEN SIBBALD   36

    SALVATION ARMY CAMP   38

    DE LA SALLE CAMP   40

    RED BARN THEATRE   41

TRAVEL AND TRANSPORTATION   45

    STAGECOACH LINES   45

    STEAMBOATS ON THE LAKE   48

    THE TORONTO & NIPISSING RAILWAY   51

    THE LAKE SIMCOE JUNCTION RAILWAY   55

    THE RADIAL RAILWAY   57

INDUSTRY ON THE LAKE   61

    FISHING   61

    ICE-FISHING   62

    LAKE SIMCOE ICE COMPANY   64

    GREW BOATS   67

RECREATION ON THE POINT   69

BIBLIOGRAPHY   76

INDEX   77

This window was designed, and made by the seven daughters of John Graves Simcoe for their friend Susan Sibbald's new church, the original St. George's Church, built in 1838.

– ROBERT HOPKINS

ACKNOWLEDGMENTS

IT is often said that we have to leave something before we really appreciate it, and it is only now that I am working with historical and genealogical materials that I realize what a historic "gold mine" I had sitting in my own backyard when I lived at Jackson's Point. My original plan for this "gold mine" was nothing more than a listing of the area's pioneers who lay in the local cemeteries. Gradually this evolved into a general history of Jackson's and Sibbald points.

Along the road to this book, there were many who offered help and encouragement. These include Ursula and Norma of Creative Photography, who graciously reproduced many photographs in exchange for nothing more than a credit in the book. To Peter Brown, who just happened to be there to open the church for Rob and me to take pictures of the interior, and incidentally to answer more than a few dumb questions, thank you. Thanks also to Mary Brown, who identified a few faces in the old photos, making the book that much more interesting. And to Barbara Sibbald, one of the first to suggest the book,

I thank you for your encouragement, but I had no idea what a massive undertaking this would be! Tom Macdonald very trustingly loaned me his collection of postcards of Jackson's Point. These are reproduced in the book, courtesy of Norma and Ursula.

Everywhere I went I met the most encouraging and helpful people: Nina Marsden of the Georgina Historical Society, everyone at the Salvation Army Archives, Dr. Johnson of West Park Hospital, Alan McGillivray of Uxbridge-Scott Museum, and John Sibbald, who had to field more than a few questions.

To all of you, to anyone I may have forgotten to thank, and finally to Harry Stemp, the first of many to say "go for it," thank you. I hope you all enjoy the results.

*The Humber-Holland Trail linked the Town of
York with Holland Landing and Lake Simcoe.*

– FROM PERCY ROBINSON'S *TORONTO DURING THE FRENCH REGIME*

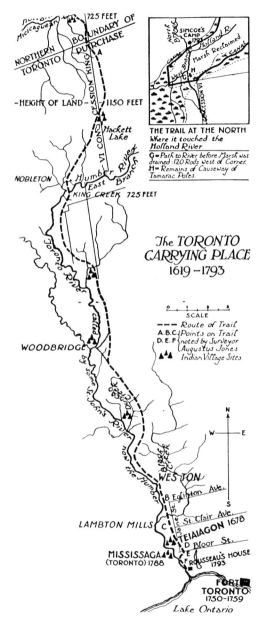

THE TRAIL AT THE NORTH
*Where it touched the
Holland River*
G = *Path to River before Marsh was
drained : 120 Rods West of Corner.*
H = *Remains of Causeway of
Tamarac Poles.*

The TORONTO
CARRYING PLACE
1619–1793

SCALE

- - - - *Route of Trail*
A.B.C. *Points on Trail*
D.E.F. *noted by Surveyor
Augustus Jones*
▲▲ *Indian Village Sites*

*When the War of 1812 ended, an anchor was abandoned near Holland Landing.
It was moved to Anchor Park in 1870.*

– FROM *LAKE SIMCOE AND ITS ENVIRONS*

THOUSANDS OF YEARS AGO, what is today Georgina Township lay at the bottom of a huge lake. As the Ice Age drew to a close, the waters began to recede, islands of land began to appear, and gradually the Oak Ridge Moraine was born.

The Oak Ridge Moraine, extending the entire width of York County, was created by the action of glaciers during a time when Canada was as cold as present-day Greenland and Antarctica. As the glaciers moved, they scraped up soil and rocks and carried them southward, dumping them in a long ridge. The area north of the Oak Ridge, which is flatter, with more bogs and swamps among dense cedar and birch bush, is called the Lake Simcoe Plain. The native people of the area used the rivers and narrow pathways through the bush and swamp to transport themselves and their furs to the trading posts on the Humber River.

Until the arrival of the English in the late 1700s, what later became south-central Ontario was very thinly populated. A few French explorers had travelled the waterways and the trails, and, in all likelihood, the first European to see Lake Simcoe, in August 1615, was Samuel de Champlain (1572–1635). He was probably led to the north end of the lake by Huron natives, although his guide and interpreter on this trip to recruit Huron to fight against the Iroquois was Étienne Brûlé, a young Frenchman who had adopted the Huron and their way of life. Perhaps Brûlé had first viewed the lake from the south, as it was likely he who was the first European to see Lakes Ontario, Huron, and Superior.

The first English-speaking traveller to see Lake Simcoe is reputed to have been Alexander Henry (1739–1824), who, while a captive of the natives at Ste Marie Among the Hurons, had accompanied them to Niagara in 1764.

Lake Simcoe has had many names. The earliest came from the Ojibwa: *Quentaron* or *Quentironk* meant "a beautiful lake"; *Ashuniong* or *Shain-e-ong* meant "silver lake." In 1888 an elderly member of the Mississauga tribe told a historian that *Ashuniong* meant "the place of the dog call." He related a legend that the lake was named "one calm day when an Indian brave stood beside the lake and thought he heard someone calling a dog named Ashunium." The voice could be heard very plainly, but there was no one to be seen, so it was thought that a spirit had been heard. The lake then became known as the "Lake of the Dog Call."

Other names included *Lac aux Claies* — "Lake of the Stakes," referring to the natives' unique method of catching fish at the narrows between Lakes Simcoe and Couchiching — and, surprisingly, "Toronto." This last name followed the sighting of the lake by Louis-Armand, Baron de la

Hontan (1666–1715) in 1687. He called it *Lac Tarontau*, meaning "a gateway" or "pass."

In 1791 Canada was divided into two provinces. The name given to the western settlements was Upper Canada, while the eastern section was called Lower Canada (for its position "lower down" the St. Lawrence River). John Graves Simcoe (1752–1806), a retired naval officer, was appointed Upper Canada's first lieutenant-governor. Simcoe moved the seat of government from Niagara to York (later renamed Toronto) in 1793, and soon after, he heard rumours about a trail connecting Lake Ontario with the upper Great Lakes. This trail had long been used by natives and early fur traders as a portage route to reach Lake Simcoe by way of what is now the Humber River. John Simcoe had an astute military mind and, sensing that American control of shipping on the Great Lakes was a possibility, he understood that an inland military route ensuring safe transport of troops and supplies throughout the province was a priority. Therefore, he located the head of this trail and set his Queen's Rangers to work building a road between the two major waterways.

On September 25, 1793, John Simcoe set out with the Queen's Rangers to explore this link between York and the upper Great Lakes. Alexander MacDonell (d. 1835), Sheriff of the Home District (the Counties of York and Peel), kept the diaries, while Alexander Aitken (d. 1799) did the actual surveying.

The party travelled on horseback as far as the end of the Carrying Place trail, which took them to the west branch of the Holland River (named for Samuel Holland [1728–1801], Canada's first surveyor-general). From there, five canoes were used to traverse the shallow swamplands of the river and reach the open waters of Lake Simcoe. In keeping with his dislike for native names, Simcoe immedi-

ately renamed this lake in honour of his father, Captain John Graves Simcoe of the Royal Navy, who had died of pneumonia in 1759 while en route to Quebec City. The Pine Fort, near today's Holland Landing, was renamed Gwillimbury after his wife Elizabeth's father, Thomas Gwillim (d. 1766), a distinguished soldier and aide-de-camp to General Wolfe at the Battle of the Plains of Abraham in Quebec. Within three years, the Pine Fort — Gwillimbury — had been connected by a cart road with the harbour at York. This track was called the Yonge military road, after Sir George Yonge (1731–1812), Britain's Secretary of War at the time.

It didn't take long for a village to spring up on the site of the Old Soldiers' Landing, also known as Steamboat Landing. The village, Holland Landing, was settled first in 1802, and ten years later, during the War of 1812, it became the port of arrival of all heavy goods coming over the portage trails and waterways between Lakes Huron and Ontario. A half-mile downstream, a lower landing was created when the Holland River proved too narrow for the larger steamers.

Anchor Park in Holland Landing is named for the massive four-thousand-pound anchor resting there. This anchor was cast in England and shipped to Canada to be used on a gunboat built during the War of 1812 at Penetanguishene, then the military headquarters of Upper Canada. The anchor arrived at York and was hauled up the Yonge military road by sixteen yoke of oxen. It moved understandably slowly, and, by 1814, when hostilities between Britain and the United States ceased, it had reached only as far as Soldiers' Bay. It was abandoned there because the navy yard at Penetanguishene was closed down, and there it languished until 1870, when it was moved to its present site, Anchor Park.

After the war between Great Britain and the United States ended in 1814, many of the young British soldiers who had fought in it chose to remain in Canada. There was not much in their homeland to entice them back; Britain was in the throes of an economic depression, and not many careers were open to ex-naval or army officers and men. Many of those who stayed were granted lands to farm north of the Town of York, some as far north as the shores of Lake Simcoe. Major William Kingdom Rains, William and James Bourchier, and John Comer were among those who settled there.

Georgina Township, named by Governor Simcoe in honour of King George III (1738–1820), was laid out in 1817 by Duncan McDonald. The first patents, or land grants, were issued in 1819. Settlement of the township was slow because of the difficulties of transportation: A journey up Yonge Street to Holland Landing, followed by a voyage across Lake Simcoe, seemed to be the only route to Georgina's lands. Settlements first developed among the dense forests beside the waterways: Udora, Egypt, Baldwin, and Virginia. Sutton and Pefferlaw on the Black River were major settlements.

Because Lake Simcoe was the "highway to the upper lakes" and the major water route across the province, Governor Simcoe felt that the capital of Upper Canada should be on its shores. The site chosen was picked for its complete protection from American waters and for the fact that it was easily accessible by steamer from Holland Landing. In 1818 the government bought the land from James Roach for $900. Roach had received his Crown land grant for Lot 22, Concessions 2 and 3, Georgina Township, and now his land was the proposed site of the capital of Upper Canada.

The government town was to be laid out in the same grid pattern as was the Town of York, but, as it turned out, the government officials and their families were quite happy to be settled at York, having made the move from Niagara only twenty years earlier. The government land at Roach's Point was eventually sold.

Settlement of the Township of Georgina began in earnest around 1826. The second wave of settlers arriving at this time tried to establish fine country-farm estates. Many were upper-class British immigrants who built vast manor houses, barns, stables, and workers' lodgings on the shores of the lake. These were more than a little too grandiose for the surrounding wilderness and rugged country.

The County of York was created in 1850 under Robert Baldwin's Municipal Act, passed the year before. When Ontario County was organized in 1852, Georgina Township became part of that county, with James O'Brien Bourchier serving on the County Council. Meetings were held in Whitby.

Charles Henry Howard, the first reeve of Georgina Township, preferred that Georgina be united with Toronto, in York County. He pushed for this to happen, and so it did; the act was passed, and it received royal assent on April 22, 1853.

Sutton became a police village in 1877 and a village in 1890. Each village or town had its own government until January 1, 1971, when the Region of York Act united them under the Townships of North Gwillimbury and Georgina. The present Town of Georgina was created on July 1, 1986.

JOHN MILLS JACKSON

JACKSON'S POINT was named for John Mills Jackson (1764?–1836), anti-government author and crusader. John Jackson was born on the island of St. Vincent in the Caribbean, the son of Dr. Josiah Jackson and Elizabeth Gerald. He went to England to attend Balliol College at Oxford University. After graduating in 1783, he returned to the island, and four years later was appointed aide-de-camp to Drewry Ottley, Governor of the West Indies. In 1795 there was an uprising by the Carib Indians, and Jackson, claiming to have lost "a considerable portion" of his land, returned to England. Having earlier bought some land in Lower Canada, he decided in 1805 to visit and inspect it. He found himself much more interested in the development of Upper Canada, and, before returning to England, he bought some land in Deer Park and Newton Brook, north of the Town of York.

John Jackson came back to Upper Canada the following year and petitioned the Executive Council for a land grant, intending to settle there permanently. The grant was refused; Jackson had associated himself in short order with Justice Robert Thorpe, Surveyor-General Charles Burton Wyatt, Joseph Willcocks, and William Weekes, and all of these men were opposed to the "Family Compact," the elite group who were running the government. Thus, although Surveyor-General Burton did his best by describing Jackson to the government as "a gentleman of respectability," it did no good. Jackson was damned by the company he kept.

Worse was to follow. At a party held in the Jackson home in the fall of that year, the liquor flowed freely and eventually the conversation turned to politics. When some of the guests tried to object to the criticisms being levelled against the government, Jackson burst out with the statement that the Upper Canadian government was "a damned rascal, surrounded by that damned Scotch faction" — alluding to the Family Compact. He went on to say that the Executive Council had "plundered the country." When a few

ONTARIO ARCHIVES   ACC. 2624-13

outraged guests left, they were followed by the host's parting shots: "Damn the governor and the government; push about the bottle!" Rumours of this party eventually reached the ears of Lieutenant-Governor Francis Gore (1769–1852), who immediately took punitive action. Justice Robert Thorpe and Surveyor-General Charles Wyatt were suspended from their offices in the House of Assembly, while Joseph Willcocks was dismissed as Sheriff of the Home District.

Jackson continued to criticize the government, alleging that compensation for the United Empire Loyalists and for those in military service seemed always to be the prime land locations. He also complained that while one-seventh of the land had been set aside for churches, no congregations had yet been organized. He opined that governing a colony in this manner could only result in a revolution.

Though most of his friends had lost their posts or were in prison, Jackson managed to escape both, probably thanks to his excellent connections — his younger brother was a member of the British Parliament. At one point, notwithstanding connections, John was about to be charged with libel, but it was decided not to lay charges when Jackson agreed to return to England of his own accord.

Back in England in 1807, Jackson wrote a letter to Lord Castlereagh, the Foreign Secretary, in which he related a few grievances found during his stay in Upper Canada. Receiving no action, or reaction, Jackson enlarged the letter into a pamphlet entitled "A View of the Political Situation in the Province of Upper Canada," published in London in 1809. In it, he charged that all the government officials in Canada had taken the best lands; that "in laying out the townships, had kept for themselves the most favourable, fertile, and salubrious places." He also went on to explain how the most "loyal, attached, and determined people had become so aggrieved, enslaved, and irritated" that they were on the verge of a revolution. He cited "impolitic and tyrannical proceedings," pointing out the "ruinous expenditure and mismanagement of public money" that had characterized much of the government of Upper Canada. Grievances of the Six Nations tribes and of military and Loyalist claimants for free land (including himself) were given as illustrations of the frustration with imperial policy.

In England, the pamphlet did not receive much attention, but when copies arrived in York, it set off a political tempest. Chief Justice William Dummer Powell tried to dismiss the document as the work of a man with only a passing acquaintance with the colony, whose "channel of information was a wretched faction of disappointed malcontents." Lieutenant-Governor Francis Gore assumed that the suspended Justice Robert Thorpe was the real author of the piece.

John Mills Jackson followed his pamphlet to Canada the next year, and in 1811 he opened a general store on Yonge Street just north of Drewry Avenue.

In 1816 he ran unsuccessfully for election in the riding of York East, and the following year he decided to relocate. Springfield Farm, his home at Newton Brook, proved difficult to sell, and once more Jackson petitioned the Executive Council for a land grant. This time his request was denied because he had "associated and identified himself with a faction whose conduct led to their suspension and removal from office."

When Springfield Farm finally sold in 1828, John Mills Jackson bought Frying-Pan Point in Georgina Township from his daughter Amelia's husband, Captain William Bourchier. Here he built himself a comfortable log cabin and lived in it until 1836, when, during a visit to England, he died. This point of land became known as Jackson's Point.

WILLIAM BOURCHIER

The first patent, or land grant, to be issued in the Township of Georgina was to Captain William Bourchier (1791–1844) in 1819. William Bourchier had come to Canada to serve with the British navy on the Great Lakes during the War of 1812. After the war ended, Captain Bourchier received a grant of twelve hundred acres on the shores of Lake Simcoe. His lands included the townsites of Sutton and Jackson's Point.

William lived with his brother James in a log cabin until April of 1821, when he married Amelia Jackson. In August of that year, William sold most of his land to his brother, and he and Amelia left the country to pursue a career in India. Amelia died during their time in India, and the couple's only child, Eustace Fane Bourchier (1822–1902), later joined the Royal Engineers.

After William died on January 22, 1844, his second wife, Laura Preston, stayed at the Point only rarely, and in 1872 she sold the land and the house built on it to Frank Sibbald.

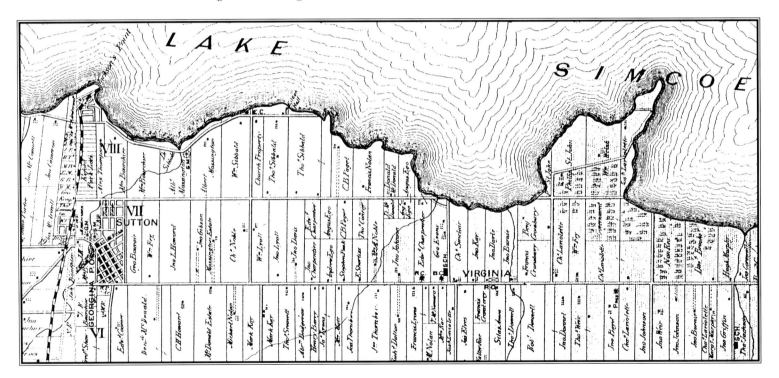

This map records the early landowners in Concessions 7 and 8, Georgina Township, between Jackson's and Sibbald points in 1878.

– HISTORICAL ATLAS OF THE COUNTY OF YORK, 1878. COURTESY OF URSULA LIANE

James O'Brien Bourchier (1797–1872), like his older brother William, served in the British navy before coming to Upper Canada. James was only twenty-one years old in 1819 when William requested a land grant for him.

Two years later, James married Jean Lyall, and the newlyweds moved to his own property in Lot 1, Concession 7 of Georgina Township, where he built a log cabin. He also constructed a dam across the Black River about two miles upstream from the lake and built a sawmill, a grist mill, and a general store. This formed the core of the little village of Bourchier's Mills, now known as Sutton West.

When Georgina's first post office opened in his store, James Bourchier served as the first postmaster, a position he eventually handed over to son John. In 1826 James Bourchier was appointed pathmaster for the area, looking after the roads, and in 1829 he was made Justice of the Peace, a post his brother William had held ten years earlier. As Justice of the Peace, James actively supported the colonial government during the Rebellion of 1837.

By 1840 James and Jean had lost their log shanty to fire and had built themselves a "manor house." When this house and the grist mill were also destroyed by fire, James, Jean, and their two sons and seven daughters moved in above the general store. James rebuilt the grist mill a few years later, and then built a new house, called The Manor. This fine red-brick house in the "Loyalist Georgian style," featured a large verandah and a kitchen wing with a bell tower. Bourchier rang the bell several times a day to inform his men that it was time to start or stop work in the fields. That bell served as the town clock for many years. In 1955 the bell, which had been cast in England around 1845, was donated to Knox United Church in Sutton.

The Manor was equipped with a private schoolroom for the Bourchier children and their friends. Two sisters of Stephen Leacock, whose family lived in nearby Egypt, attended school here.

As early as 1846 James Bourchier had begun selling off hundred-acre lots from his land holdings, and seven years later he laid out the village of Bourchier's Mills in its present form. The plan, like that of Toronto and Roach's Point, was a grid pattern with squares for market, school, and churches. To further settle his village, Bourchier began to sell off one-acre lots along the roads. In 1851 the village contained the grist mill and a sawmill, a carding and fulling mill, a tannery, and a cloth factory. By 1853 a two-storey mill was built beside the river across High Street (the village's main road) from James's general store and post office.

The general store had become a cheese factory by 1900, and in 1904 it was bricked over and used as the town hall. The general store, built of logs on a three-foot stone foundation, had actually been constructed to face onto the Black River. It featured a "river door," open to native traders and other travellers on the Black River. As High Street was developed, however, the storefront was relocated to meet the customers arriving by horse and wagon.

Both James and William Bourchier were active in the establishment of church and school. The first schoolhouse in Sutton was built in 1842, and the building also served as the church and as the town meeting hall. The idea for a church in Sutton was opposed, as it was felt that the Anglican Church at Sibbald Point was sufficient.

James O'Brien Bourchier died on August 20, 1872, at The Manor, and the flag of the York Pioneers' Association, of which he had been an active member, was flown at half-mast atop the St. Lawrence Market in Toronto in his honour.

WILLIAM JOHNSON

Captain William Johnson (1784–1851), the son of William Johnstone and Jean Fife, was born at Chirnside, Scotland, and came to Georgina in 1819. Upon joining the British navy at the age of seventeen, William had been made to shorten his surname to Johnson.

Young William served at the sieges of Cadiz and Tarragon in Spain during the Napoleonic Wars, and by 1813 he had reached the rank of lieutenant. After the Battle of Waterloo and the end of the war, Johnson retired on half-pay. Like many other ex-naval officers at the time, William Johnson had trouble finding work in Britain, so he accepted a land grant in Upper Canada — Lot 6, Concession 7, Georgina Township — and set sail for the Canadas.

After three months at sea, William landed at Montreal, walked from there to York and then north to his land on Lake Simcoe. When he reached his lot east of the present town of Sutton, Johnson set to and built himself a primitive log cabin. He called his new home Oldcastle.

During the early 1820s, Johnson tried to establish a mill at Baldwin, but before the mill and dam could be completed, a severe storm and flood swept everything away. William was thinking of rebuilding when one day his cow wandered off into the bush. While looking for her, he came upon a large, fast-flowing river, the Black River, and made note of the fine timber in the area. Johnson bought this piece of land, then wrote to his brother in Scotland asking for money so that he could build a new sawmill. Along with the money, his brother sent a suggestion that he call his new mill town Pefferlaw, the name of a field on the family farm in Scotland.

By the mid-1820s, the sawmill was built and William was busy clearing his land to prepare for a family. He married Roxanna Smalley, whose family had settled in the Cook's Bay area. William later built a school on his property for the couple's nine children.

By 1832 William Johnson had added grist and woollen mills to his sawmill, and the little village of Pefferlaw was growing. The following year, his brother Robert Johnstone immigrated to Canada and built the village's first general store where, in 1851, the Pefferlaw post office opened.

William was appointed a magistrate and Justice of the Peace. He sat on the Council for the Home District (the County of York), and was a friend and supporter of the Rebel leader William Lyon Mackenzie, who visited the Johnson home on many occasions. Indeed, after the Rebellion of 1837, when Mackenzie was forced to flee to the United States, Johnson visited him there. The friendship did not endear Johnson to the other settlers in the area — the Bourchiers, Mossingtons, and Sibbalds — who were all supporters of the establishment Family Compact and the government.

William Johnson died on March 28, 1851, at Oldcastle, and he was buried beside his wife, a son, and a daughter in a private graveyard on the property.

The little village of Pefferlaw grew rapidly after railway lines were built in 1906 between Toronto and Sudbury by the Canadian National Railway Company.

John Comer (1782–1856) came to Upper Canada in 1814 on the same ship that carried William and James Bourchier. Like the Bourchiers, John Comer had been a military man; in his case, serving with the British army during the Napoleonic Wars.

In 1822 John Comer was granted Lot 5, Concession 7 in Georgina Township, and he settled down on the shores of Lake Simcoe on the farm later known as Rotherwood.

John and Margaret Comer were the parents of the first white child to be born in Georgina Township. When Elizabeth Georgina Comer was born, on August 9, 1818, King George III granted her a lot of her own on Concession 7. When Elizabeth grew up, she married Mark Mossington, son of another area pioneering family. Mark, fourteen years Elizabeth's junior, died in 1857 when he was only twenty-five years old. Elizabeth lived on, leading, in the words of friends, "a life full of strength and activity" until 1917. She was ninety-nine years old.

John Comer, who was appointed Georgina's first assessor and tax collector, donated five acres of his land in 1837 for a churchyard and cemetery, now the site of St. George's Anglican Church on Sibbald Point.

Mossington's sawmill at the mouth of the Black River around 1910.

The land bought by Thomas Mossington (1780–1864), Lots 4 and 5 on Concession 8 in Georgina Township, included property to the west of the mouth of the Black River and known as Land's End. Land's End was the name given to any spot where the forests were so dense that from either the water or the road nothing could be seen but trees.

Thomas Mossington, a lumber agent for the British navy, had first seen Canada in 1804 when he was sent to inspect timber and to locate good, tall, straight white pine to be used as masts for ships. He returned in 1812 to design vessels for service on the Great Lakes during the war between the United States and Great Britain. When that war ended in 1814, Mossington went home to England, then spent ten years based in Venice and travelling around Europe buying timber and other supplies for the fleets.

In 1829 Thomas and his family immigrated to Upper Canada. After a rough two-month-long ocean crossing, the Mossington family were content to settle for a while at Quebec City, but Thomas and his son Ian soon set out to find their land on Lake Simcoe. They travelled by *bateaux* (flat-bottomed boats) down the St. Lawrence River and through Lake Ontario to York. From there a stagecoach took them to Newmarket and Holland Landing, where they hired a boat and four men to ferry them to their property near Jackson's Point. Here, the two men stayed with John Comer and his family.

The Mossingtons had bought the farm of John Peregrine, who had decided to move further south to land just west of today's Woodbine Avenue and north of the Ravenshoe Road. The Mossington farm consisted of a hundred and seventy acres — forty of them already cleared and fenced by John Peregrine. There was a small frame house on the property, which Mossington called Plumstead, for his

home in England. In later years, the Mossingtons bought the adjoining two hundred acres.

Thomas Mossington soon became an active member of his new community. Within a year, he had been appointed a magistrate of Georgina Township. He became known for his fair and impartial decisions, and the dining room of Plumstead served as a county courtroom. In 1832 he became one of the shareholders of the *Simcoe*, the first steamer to sail on the lake. As one of the first wardens of St. George's Church, Thomas laid out the plans and built a wooden model of the proposed church, then oversaw its construction in 1838.

As a magistrate, Thomas Mossington was instrumental in putting down the Rebellion of 1837, and he made sure Plumstead was ready for any eventuality. A unique feature of the Mossington home was a trap-door in the floor, leading to a tunnel to the lakeshore, where a boat lay waiting in case there was a need for a fast escape from a rebel attack. Guns were strategically placed along the front of the house.

Mary Ann, Thomas's wife, died in 1835. Six years later, Thomas married Martha Donnell, a girl much younger than himself. This occasion was marked by a shivaree, a noisy mock serenade given a newlywed couple on their first night together in their new home. We have John Sibbald's description of this celebration from his diary of January 5, 1841:

Mr. Mossington, one of our neighbours, an old gentleman with a numerous family, married a Miss Donnell, aged 21. The people at Sutton and Bourchier's Mills concluded they would give him a Shivaree, a Canadian custom. All the idlers, loafers, and blackguards about a township repair to the newly married couple's house at night and serenade them with sleigh bells, cow bells, and every other noisy article they can lay hold of, and shout and make a row until the persecuted husband bribes them to go away by giving them some liquor. About thirty of them, boys and men, headed, they say, by Mr. Corbett in a female dress, assembled at 10 P.M. at the old Mossington's and kicked up an infernal row enough to waken seven sleepers. Old Mossington, who does everything methodically, came and tried to identify the parties in case they might do any harm. He told them he would give them an order on the tavern at the Mill for a gallon of whiskey if they should go away. They complied at first, but after pocketing the order, they said they must drink his health there, so he was obliged to fork out four bottles more before they would depart in peace.

After Thomas Mossington died, on March 9, 1864, the family farm was taken over by his sons: Moses (1813–95), Thomas (1817–96), and Albert Edward (1843–1919). Albert built the Mossington Mill at the mouth of the Black River. Sawed logs floated down the Black from the region's dense pine forests. The lumber was used to build houses and barns in the area. The mill was operated by steam power, and the smokestack was often used as a marker by boats out on the lake.

The present Mossington bridge over the wide and shallow Black River was built in 1912, using hand-mixed cement. The willows and marshy lands were dredged out, and winds off the lake soon had the flatlands covered with sand.

Young Thomas Mossington built the present home at Plumstead in 1886, incorporating the original cabin into the new house. The fine frame-and-stucco dwelling included a kitchen wing and a bell tower. When Thomas Jr. became a trustee of the first school in the area, one of the rooms in the house was used as a classroom, and Miss Minnie Sibbald was the teacher. As in the old house, the dining room doubled as a courtroom after Thomas was appointed a county magistrate.

A listing in the 1989 directory, two years after Thomas Jr.'s death, lists Plumstead as "one of the most popular private boarding houses of Jackson's Point, able to accommodate up to twenty guests." Plumstead, the area's oldest house, remained in the Mossington family until 1974, when it was purchased by George and Catherine Burns. Today it is still a "popular private boarding house," as they operate a bed and breakfast in their home.

SIMON LEE

Simon Lee had worked for the East India Company before moving to Upper Canada and settling at Thornhill in 1832. Here he built a large, plantation-style, two-storey frame house on Yonge Street before moving further north around 1835 and settling on Lot 8, Concession 8 in Georgina Township. His five hundred acres of land included property just east of what is now Sibbald Point Provincial Park.

Simon Lee was secretary of the group set up to look into the building of an Anglican church in Georgina. St. George's Anglican Church was built near his home in 1838.

Emily Buxton Lee, Simon's oldest daughter, married William Sibbald of Eildon Hall. William had really wanted to marry the Lee's second daughter, Mary Ready, but Mrs. Lee and tradition stated that the girls in a family had to marry in order of age, and, as William was the first to ask, he was obliged to marry Emily. The groom had to be enticed to the altar "with liberal portions of brandy," but the marriage turned out to be a happy one, although short; the bride died on April 8, 1854, at the young age of twenty-eight.

Mary Ready Lee married John Barwick of Thornhill and the couple moved into her father's big house on Yonge Street, where they raised eighteen children. A third Lee daughter, Eliza, married Captain Robert Douglas Stupart of the Royal Navy.

William Kingdom Rains (sometimes spelled Raines) was born in Wales in 1789, just four weeks after the beginning of the French Revolution. He was only sixteen years old when he received his commission as a lieutenant in the Royal Regiment of Artillery. From 1807 until 1813, William fought in Europe in the Peninsular War. For his part in the war, and in recognition of his brilliant military career, Major Rains was made a Knight of the Grand Cross of the Order of Leopold by Francis I of Austria.

After the war ended, William Rains retired on half-pay and settled for a time on the family estate in Wales, Sutton Lodge, before moving to England, where he practised engineering. However, he missed the excitement of military life, and in 1824 he rejoined the army and was sent to Malta. While there, Rains saw an officer poring over maps of America, and he became fascinated with the delineations of the various waterways and their relationships to the Great Lakes. He was especially interested in the St. Mary's River connecting Lakes Superior and Huron. Rains decided to visit that area, perhaps even to make his home there.

William dreamed of setting up a colony in the new land, and in order to fulfil his dream, he sold his commission and set out for Upper Canada. In the early 1820s, he was granted Lot 7, Concession 9 in Georgina, and within three years he had built three houses, including one for himself that he called Penn Range.

William Rains was described by contemporaries as a "jovial gentleman, notorious for his success with the fairer sex." On his voyage across the Atlantic, he met up with sixteen-year-old Frances Doubleday and her younger sister Eliza, the daughters of his friend Jack (Mad Jack) Doubleday. When the girls lost both parents, the debonair Rains "came to their rescue." First, Frances moved into Penn Range with him, and shortly thereafter they were joined by Eliza. Frances produced thirteen children and Eliza seven, all fathered by William Rains, who had left five children and their mother behind in England.

In 1834 Rains proposed to the government of Upper Canada that he be granted land on St. Joseph Island in Lake Huron. Rains planned to settle one hundred families there and set up his colony. Sir John Colborne (1778–1863), then Lieutenant-Governor of Upper Canada, was supportive of Rains's scheme — not surprising as he was a fellow veteran of the Napoleonic Wars — but he could not grant him such a large tract of land. Thus Rains was allowed to "purchase" five thousand acres of land at a shilling an acre.

Around this time Susan Sibbald arrived in Upper Canada and bought Penn Range and its surrounding land from William Rains. William, Frances, Eliza, and their children moved to St. Joseph Island, where Rains built a separate house for each of his families.

Now Rains and a group of investors set out to colonize the island. One of the partners owned the new Georgian Bay steamer *Penetanguishene*, and it was decided that the boat would be the supply vessel for their enterprise. That spring, they loaded up the ship with merchandise and machinery. A sawmill was established on the island, and Rains and company were ready for the arrival of settlers who would use their businesses to build homes. However, by 1839 the little settlement had only eight houses. The rest of the province was opening up and land was free, so it seemed foolish for people to travel the distance to an island where they had to pay for the land.

Within two years, Rains had dropped out of the company.

Others sold their shares until only one remained. A report made to the government in 1840 stated that no new settlers had come, but that Charles Thompson, who still operated the boat, had shipped out upwards of six hundred barrels of fish and a "full one million pounds of maple sugar." The sugar alone had a market value of over $75,000!

William Rains continued to live on St. Joseph Island with his wives and children. Anna Jameson visited them in 1837 and wrote in her diary: "There is, in the interior, an English settlement and a village of Indians. The principal proprietor, Major R ——, who is magistrate and justice of the peace, has two . . . women living with him — two sisters, and a family by each! — such are the examples sometimes set to the Indians on our frontiers!"

Enjoying a sleigh ride in front of Sibbald House around 1900.

– GEORGINA HISTORICAL SOCIETY POSTCARD COLLECTION

*Susan and
Betsy Isabella Mein.*
– MEMOIRS OF
SUSAN SIBBALD, COURTESY
OF URSULA LIANE

Susan Sibbald (1783–1866), who bought Penn Range from William Kingdom Rains in 1835, had come to Upper Canada to investigate rumours that two of her sons, William and Charles, were living "riotously" above a tavern in Orillia.

Susan had been born in Cornwall, England, the fifth daughter of Royal Navy surgeon Thomas Mein, a well-known patron of the arts, literature, and music. After he retired, the Mein family moved to their ancestral home, Eildon Hall, near Melrose, Scotland.

Susan Mein was "launched into society" in 1800 at the age of seventeen. She and one of her sisters, Betsy Isabella, attended house parties and military balls in both London and Edinburgh, joining a world of fine art and literature, politics, and army and navy life. Poems were written in their honour, and their portraits were hung in the Royal Academy. A miniature of Susan was created by Henry Bone, enameller to King George III and a friend of the Mein family.

In 1806 Susan met a British army colonel on leave in Scotland. She was immediately captivated by William Sibbald's (1771–1835) "elegant manner," and within a year of their meeting, Susan and William were married.

Susan and William had eleven children; nine sons and two daughters. Five sons served in the Royal Navy, one served with the army in India, and two eventually jointed the militia in Canada.

In 1833, on the advice of a friend, Sir John Colborne, Lieutenant-Governor of Upper Canada, William sent two of his sons to the new land to learn farming. William Jr. and Charles were apprenticed to Clifford Thompson of Orillia. After a few months, news trickled back that the boys were living above a tavern; someone even reported that they had been seen drinking. Susan Sibbald decided that she wanted to see for herself just what was going on.

William was too ill at the time to accompany his wife, so Susan took another son, Archibald, along for company. Arriving at Orillia on the steamer from Holland Landing, Susan found her sons to be doing very well — being, in fact, "industrious and prosperous." In those early days of Upper Canada, living above a tavern was considered quite respectable, since the inns and taverns were often the only places where people could stay until their own shanties or houses were built.

Susan took advantage of the long trip by touring around Orillia and Lake Simcoe. She was so taken with the beauty of the countryside and the dense forests that she decided she wanted to live here. During a summer boat ride she discovered Penn Range which, along with five hundred acres of land, was for sale, and in the fall of 1835 she bought the Rains farm and buildings, which included a box-shaped house with many chimneys, styled after a British officer's cottage. Susan, William, and Charles moved into their new home on November 17, 1835, and one of her first acts was to tear down a tavern which had stood on the property.

As soon as the ice broke up the following spring, Susan and Archibald left for England. Happy with her new home,

Susan was looking forward to a new life in Canada with her husband and family, but when she reached Britain, she learned that her husband, William, had died while on duty in India. A letter announcing his death had reached Georgina in March, just after Susan had left Canada.

Susan settled her affairs in England, left Archibald to enlist in the Royal Navy, and returned to Penn Range, now Eildon Hall, to start a new life. She arrived at Lake Simcoe in October 1835, bringing with her her three youngest sons: Hugh, Francis, and Ogilvie.

Like many other British immigrants who could afford to do so, Susan wanted to bring with her elements of the fine lifestyle she had enjoyed at home. Among the possessions she brought were a grandfather clock, settees, naval chests, curio cabinets, chairs, tables, and four cast-iron stoves. In keeping with her love of art, literature, and elegance, Susan also brought portraits, books, china, silver, and fine linens and clothing. After two boat trips, everything was loaded onto ox-carts and hauled up Yonge Street to Holland Landing to be shipped across the lake to Jackson's Point.

At Eildon Hall, many of the old-world customs relating to class and status were maintained. The family had a stable of fine horses, and carriages for them to pull; there were servants to cook, tenant farmers to cultivate the land, and gardeners to look after the estate gardens of shade trees and exotic shrubs. Thomas Sibbald brought many plants and seedlings from around the world. The Italian weeping ash, still flourishing in front of Eildon Hall, was brought from Italy as a seedling in a flowerpot around 1850.

Eildon Hall was described as the most aristocratic home in this part of the country. Peacocks strutted arrogantly on the spacious, well-kept lawns. Although built of wood, the house itself had the appearance of stone. Inside, it was papered and carpeted, and, with the fine furniture and artifacts brought by Susan, could offer family and visitors every European comfort.

Thomas Sibbald, known as "Captain Tom," was a good friend to the natives on Georgina Island. A Christmas tradition during Captain Tom's time at Eildon Hall was that on Christmas night natives from the islands would cross the lake bearing gifts for the Sibbald family. Buffalo robes were kept at the house in case anyone had to spend the night there due to storms on the lake. Christmas, which often included sons on leave from various parts of the world, was celebrated in true English fashion.

But, by the late 1840s, with farm workers demanding higher wages and the traditional British ways of farming proving to be unprofitable, Susan and her sons gave up Eildon Hall as a working farm. Susan returned to England, while William and Thomas pursued other careers in the area.

In 1850 Susan returned to Canada and lived in Toronto until her death at the age of eighty-three. She is buried in the family plot beside St. George's Church.

William Sibbald, who had married Simon Lee's eldest daughter, Emily, built a home just east of the church, which he called Rotherwood. William lived at Rotherwood until 1877, when the house was taken over by his niece's husband, Charles Berkeley Paget.

Thomas Sibbald retired from the navy to live in Eildon Hall with his wife and family, bringing with him in 1856 his navy batman, John Metheral, known affectionately as "Old John." John and his family were the first inhabitants of a cottage that much later became known as the Indian House. Given this name in 1910 because native families employed on the estate lived there, this cottage still stands in Sibbald Point Provincial Park.

Eildon Hall and the Indian House remained in the Sibbald family until 1951, when they were purchased by the County of York to be transformed into a park. The land was taken over by the Province of Ontario in 1956 and renamed Sibbald Point Provincial Park. After much restoration and renovation, Eildon Hall opened as a museum in 1959.

St. George's Church as it appears today on the shores of Lake Simcoe.

– ROBERT HOPKINS

AFTER SUSAN SIBBALD settled in the area, one of her priorities was to arrange for the building of a church. To this end, she donated sixty-six acres of land on the lakeshore for a church and cemetery. Five more acres were donated by a neighbour, John Comer. With the help of John Mills Jackson, Susan started a subscription for the building, contributing the largest amount, £ 50, herself. Another neighbour, Jackson's son-in-law William Bourchier, contributed a raft of lumber.

In 1835 the Bourchiers, Jacksons, Mossingtons, and Sibbalds petitioned Lieutenant-Governor John Colborne for land to be used for a school, church, and burial ground. By February 1837 the schoolhouse had been built. Next came the church. It was a long struggle. The Church of England hierarchy was slow to respond, the Bishop of Quebec offered no assistance, and the Anglican Church of Canada finally donated all of £ 25. Other money and materials were collected from neighbours, friends, and relatives in Canada and England.

The name St. George's was decided upon for the church, suggested by Susan Sibbald for the patron saint of England, whom she greatly admired. Thomas Mossington had built a wooden model of the church, and he oversaw its construction. The original building stood just to the

St. George's Church as it appeared in the 1930s. In 1935 cracks began to appear in the tower walls and the small tower on top of the main tower was removed under the direction of Captain W. Wallace. The present tower is six feet shorter than the original, pictured here.

– FROM THE MEMOIRS OF SUSAN SIBBALD, COURTESY OF URSULA LIANE north of the present church. It was begun on May 25, 1838, and by August 15 the framework was completed, and an entry in the diary of William Sibbald noted: "Day warm and fine. We all went to a bee for the raising of the church. There were twenty-nine people present."

The Reverend John Gibson (1801–52) arrived in Georgina from England in June of the following year, and he and his family stayed with Susan Sibbald at Eildon Hall until the church was completed and the manse could be built. The first services of the St. George's congregation were held in the drawing room of the Sibbald house. The little church itself was officially dedicated by Bishop John Strachan (1778–1867) on August 26, 1839, although only the walls were up; there was no roof or altar and the church was described by Reverend Gibson as "a neat little church, though it is only a shell, with planks for seats, and a few boards nailed together for a pulpit." Thomas Mossington and Samuel Park were the church's first wardens.

The Simcoe family, friends of Susan and of her late husband, lent their support to St. George's. The daughters of Governor Simcoe and his wife, Elizabeth, created a glass window for the Sibbald church. The window features seven crosses, representing the seven Simcoe sisters. It was shipped to Georgina in pieces, entrusted to a traveller — perhaps Susan Sibbald herself — and arrived happily intact. After reconstruction, it was placed in the little wooden church.

When Susan Sibbald died, in 1866, her sons wanted to build a larger, more permanent church in her memory, and it took ten years to prepare for the construction of this much grander building. In order that there be no disruption of services, the little wooden building that was the existing church was placed on rollers (probably logs) and wheeled to a new site closer to the lake.

The new church was built under the direction of Captain Thomas Sibbald, who brought many of his naval practices to the job site. Each day "at precisely eight bells," Captain Tom issued rum rations and supervised the toasting of the Queen's health. Thomas also took it upon himself to oversee the stone-cutting and -laying to ensure that no iron deposits could be detected in the stones. Only one stone slipped through his inspection, and the rusty iron stain on it can be seen on the west wall. The stones had been brought across the lake on scows from a quarry near Barrie. From the wharf at Jackson's Point, they had been transported by wagon along the lakeshore road.

The first service in the new church was held on June 10, 1877. William Ritchie (1799–1855), husband of Susan Sibbald's daughter Anne Sibbald, conducted the service. The organist was Georgina, youngest daughter of Captain Tom.

The church's interior received attention over the next few years. Much of the furnishings were fastioned from local woods: the pulpit and prayer desk are of butternut, while the Holy Table and hymn board are of oak. Much of the carving was done by the Reverend George Everest, who married a granddaughter of Susan Sibbald and who played the organ and often conducted services at St. George's from 1901 until his death in 1908. Reverend Everest was a great nephew of the Surveyor-General of India, Sir George Everest, for whom Mount Everest was named.

The Second World War greatly diminished the church's congregation through the enlistment of many of its members. After the war, it was decided to hold services at St. George's only during the summer months. Campers' services were held from 1956, when Sibbald Park opened, until 1978, when a resident park chaplaincy was established. Services are again held each Sunday morning during the months of July and August in St. George's Anglican Church, Sibbald Point.

The graves of the Sibbald family beside St. George's Church.

– ROBERT HOPKINS

ONCE THE CHURCH had been built, attention could be turned to the grounds and to the cemetery. Much of this work began after the construction of the first church and before the stone building was even planned. Cedar hedges and maple and pine trees were planted by Thomas Sibbald, who had a passion for cedar hedges. He noted in his diary: "On my arrival here [at Eildon Hall] in 1856, the fence was in such a state that animals went in and out at pleasure. In 1857, I planted the cedar hedge, the plants being so small that the children brought them from the bush in their pinafores. A neat picket fence was put up (to protect the young plants), since replaced by stone."

Like many small cemeteries in Upper Canada, St. George's was originally set aside as a family burial plot. Wandering through it today, one can not only trace family trees but can also see that more than a few prominent Ontarians lie here.

Alfred Chapman (1878–1949), for instance, was an architect whose works included two libraries, Knox College, the Harbour Commission building in Toronto, Havergal College, the Sunnyside Bathing Pavilion, and many buildings on the Exhibition grounds. Alfred Chapman and his family were cottagers, spending their summer vacations at Jackson's Point during the 1880s. John Gibson, William

Ritchie, W. I. D. Smith, and George Everest were all members of the clergy who served the parish of St. George's. For many years, Cedric Sowby, another member of the clergy, had a cottage behind The Briars.

Two famous Canadian authors, Mazo de la Roche and Stephen Leacock, and their families rest here.

Mazo de la Roche was born in 1879 at Newmarket, where her grandparents John and Sarah Roche are buried. Mazo was very fond of her grandmother Sarah, who died in 1911, and the grandmother in her Whiteoaks of Jalna series of novels closely resembles her, even sharing her birthdate.

William Roche, Mazo's father, and his brother Danford

The Leacock family on their farm near Egypt after the departure of their father, Walter Peter Leacock.
Left to right: Teddy with Gyp the family dog, Charlie, Stephen, Dot, Carrie, Mrs. Agnes Leacock, Daisy, Jim, Maymee, Missie, and George.

– NATIONAL ARCHIVES OF CANADA   C31954

operated stores in Aurora, Newmarket, and Toronto. Danford built the first telephone line in Newmarket to link his two stores. In 1884 Danford moved to Toronto to open a store on Yonge Street, leaving William to manage the Newmarket shops. The next year, William Roche stopped working for his brother and moved his family to Toronto. They moved frequently after that, before ending up at Foxleigh Farm near Bronte.

While she was living with her maternal grandparents in Parkdale, in Toronto, Mazo met her cousin Caroline Clement. Caroline soon became her closest companion and is also buried in St. George's Cemetery. Mazo and Caroline were always inventing stories, and Mazo fantasized that her family were French aristocrats who had escaped to Ireland to avoid persecution before coming to Canada. To further this fantasy, Mazo added "de la" to her surname, the only member of the family to do so.

In 1927 Mazo wrote her first Whiteoaks of Jalna novel, winning with it the *Atlantic Monthly* Fiction Award, worth $10,000. This led to fourteen sequels portraying life in nineteenth-century Ontario based on her family and her personal experiences, with many embellishments dreamed up by Mazo and Caroline.

With the success of her first novel and its stage adaptions, Mazo moved to England where, in 1931, she adopted two children, Esme and Rene. In 1939, with the outbreak of the Second World War, Mazo brought her children to Toronto. The success of her books allowed the family to live quite luxuriously in Forest Hill Village.

Mazo de la Roche spent many summers on the shores of Lake Simcoe. In fact, it was here that she learned that her first novel had been accepted for publication. Over the last five summers of her life, she was a guest at The Briars, usually staying with Caroline in Cottage No. 2, where she could write and "have her privacy respected."

On July 12, 1961, Mazo de la Roche died at her home in Toronto. She had left instructions that if she died in Canada, she was to be buried either in the Anglican church cemetery at York Mills or at Sibbald Point. She had also left instructions for Caroline to destroy all her diaries and letters. Caroline decided that her cousin should be buried in St. George's Cemetery. John Sibbald, the church warden at the time, and Mazo's son, Rene, chose the site. Because the family were not members of the church, it was arranged that a window would be dedicated in Mazo's memory.

Mazo de la Roche's gravestone, the tallest in the cemetery, features a Celtic cross, an exact replica of her grandparents' cross in the Newmarket cemetery. Caroline Clement and Rene, who died in 1984, both rest beside Mazo de la Roche.

Like Mazo de la Roche, Stephen Leacock spent many summer holidays on the shores of Lake Simcoe. His father's family had made its fortune in the wine trade in England and had belonged to the "Tory leisure class." Stephen's father, Walter Peter Leacock, chose to elope with Agnes Emma Butler and so was "banished to the colonies." The young couple made a disastrous try at life in South Africa before returning to England. Stephen was born there in 1869, seven years before the decision was made to immigrate to Canada.

Peter and his eldest son, nine-year-old Jim, came out in advance to prepare the way for the rest of the family. Agnes and her other six children sailed across the ocean on the Allan Line steamer the *Samaritan*. They docked at Montreal, took a river steamer to Toronto, then travelled to Newmarket, the nearest railway terminus to the south shore of Lake Simcoe. Peter and his hired hand, Old Tommy, met the family there and packed Agnes, children, and belongings into two horse-drawn wagons for the trek north to Egypt.

By this time (1876), the hundred-acre farm on Lot 6, Concession 4 in Georgina was pretty well established. There was a log house ("with its addition of wood, thin as cardboard and cold as a refrigerator") heated by nine stoves, as well as three barns, an implement shed, and a smoke-house. The house was lighted by coal-oil lamps.

Four more children were born while the family lived on the farm, making eleven Leacock children in all. With the financial help of their grandfather in England, the Leacock children were tutored at home by Harry Park of Sutton, and, again with his grandfather's help, at the age of thirteen, Stephen joined his brothers at Upper Canada College.

The farm was a mixed farm — wheat, hay, cattle, sheep, pigs, hens, and a market garden — but little profit was realized and it wasn't long before Peter Leacock left the family to seek his own fortune. In 1883 Agnes rented the farm to a neighbour, left the younger children with her friends William and Emily Lee Sibbald, and moved to Toronto. The Leacock farmhouse at Egypt burned down in the winter of 1960.

In 1891 Stephen graduated with a degree in political science and economics, but with his family in need of money, he became a teacher, working at Strathroy and Uxbridge high schools. This career left him his summers free to spend with his mother and younger siblings. Ever since they had left the farm, the Leacocks had spent their summers at Lake Simcoe, at first in a former rectory for which Agnes paid a yearly rent of $8, and later in a cottage rented from Jack Sibbald for $50 per year. This cottage, which stood where the Chipman house now stands, was a one-storey building with a long, narrow verandah facing the lake. Jack's son John Sibbald remembers it as being "constructed mainly of cedar poles and lined with elm bark. The verandah had cedar-pole supports painted white and the floor was typical Lake Simcoe, painted grey."

After Agnes died in 1934, the cottage was given back to the Sibbald family. When Kathleen Sibbald Lloyd, Jack Sibbald's sister, wanted to replace it with a larger cottage, the Leacock house was moved across the road to the Briars Golf Club, where it is now known as Cottage No. 9.

In 1903 Stephen joined the faculty of McGill University as its first professor in political science. Considered a pioneer political economist, Stephen Leacock wrote over sixty books. To earn extra money, he wrote humorous pieces for magazines such as *Punch* and *Saturday Night*. His first humorous book, *Literary Lapses*, was published in 1910. During the 1920s and 1930s, he also wrote a number of one-act plays.

By 1895, with most of her children grown, Agnes had moved to Orillia; she then lived for a while with her daughter at Beaverton. Around 1910 she made her home at The Grange, a white stucco house on the Sibbald estate. Finally, her children built her a "somewhat eccentric house" in Sutton. Bury Lodge, named for her childhood home in England, was Agnes's home until she died.

Stephen Leacock married Beatrix Hamilton and they had one son, Stephen Lushington Leacock. Beatrix died in England and her ashes were interred in St. James's Cemetery in Toronto. Stephen had always intended to move them to St. George's Cemetery, but never did.

With the fortune he made from writing, Stephen bought a summer home on Old Brewery Bay on Lake Couchiching. When he died on March 28, 1944, of throat cancer, he was buried in the family plot, which he had earlier described as "just to the west of Sibbald's Church, almost directly below the big stained-glass window, easy to find because of the upside-down tree." This Camperdown elm, described as an umbrella tree, has since been replaced with a weeping ash.

The Briars Country Club opened in August 1923.

– Georgina Historical Society Postcard Collection

THE BRIARS

WILLIAM BOURCHIER called his Georgina home The Briars after the house of his friend William Balcombe, with whom he had worked in the East India Company. Balcombe's Briars was on the British island of Saint Helena, about twelve hundred miles west of Africa. Napoleon had been exiled to the island of Saint Helena by the British after his defeat at Waterloo. He was to stay at Longwood, the home of the island's lieutenant-governor. Longwood, however, wasn't ready for him, and Napoleon, noticing a red-roofed bungalow set into the side of a mountain, beside a waterfall and amidst lush vegetation, asked if he could stay there until it was ready. That bungalow was The Briars, and the Balcombe family welcomed him into their home. Napoleon joined the Balcombes for parties and games and spent his happiest days on Saint Helena under their roof.

William Bourchier had also stayed at The Briars on Saint Helena, and he reproduced its gracefully arched verandah on his home at Jackson's Point. The Briars at the Point is a typical Regency-style house situated to enjoy the best view of the lake, unlike most houses of the day, which were built to sit "squarely on the roads."

After William Bourchier died in 1844, his widow stayed at The Briars only rarely, so she decided to offer the land for sale, "being within a few miles of a steamboat landing, mills, post office, and church."

Francis (Frank) Sibbald (1824–1904), one of Susan's sons, had been a medical missionary in Shanghai, and on his retirement, he wanted to establish a home fine enough for a man of his position in the area. He bought The Briars in 1872 and immediately began making plans to turn it into a working farm. He added a brick coach house, a stable, and a peacock house, importing the birds from India. He kept a herd of Holsteins in the barn (which is now the Red Barn Theatre), and built a bell-tower to be used as a time-clock for the farm workers.

Frank Sibbald shared his brother Tom's passion for hedges, and it was this that gave the road in front of his house its name, Hedge Road. He also planted many of the pine trees that line the roadway between The Briars and St. George's Church and Eildon Hall.

Frank Sibbald's first addition to the house was a service wing, connected to the main dining room by a verandah on the outside and a square opening in the dining room wall. The west wing, consisting of "two grand drawing rooms," was added around 1800 as a summer wing. The driveway between Sibbald's house and the coach house was a favourite spot for garden parties and church socials. Frank Sibbald was most generous in opening up his home for fund-raising affairs. Local musicians often provided the entertainment, while food was served by the ladies of the nearby churches.

When Frank Sibbald died unmarried in 1904, the farm was passed down to his niece Elizabeth Kemp Sibbald, and when she died in 1919, it went to John Drinkwater Sibbald (1845–1923), known as Jack. Jack Sibbald got into the hospitality business by building summer cottages along the lakeshore, which he then rented out. Jack passed the farm on to his son, John Drinkwater Sibbald II (1891–1960). In 1927, The Briars became home to its first bride when Jack Jr. married Marjorie Temple Troop.

One of the new bride's tasks was to pump the hundred-gallon water tank full each morning, as The Briars included very little in the way of modern facilities. It did have electricity, as wiring had been put in around 1920, but this was restricted to the sitting rooms, which boasted over fifty fixtures, including a crystal chandelier that had been bought at the Casa Loma auction sale. The remaining rooms, mainly bedrooms, continued to be lighted by coal-oil lamps.

The Briars Country Club dining room is used for barbecues and other summer gatherings.

– ROBERT HOPKINS

Jack Sibbald continued to operate The Briars as a working farm, and he established The Briars Dairy and Creamery to complement his Holstein herd. The creamery operated in Sutton until 1971.

Around 1940 Jack began renting out his cottages on the lake to "golfers and bridge players" as well as families. In 1942 he hired a cook and a few local girls to wait on tables and keep house, then invited his friends to come and stay as paying guests. The Briars Country Club was open for business.

When John Sibbald II died in 1960, his son, also named John, inherited the business. Although he had studied engineering, John decided that he preferred the resort trade and set out to enlarge his holdings. In 1977 extensive renovations were made to Sibbald House, and The Briars was opened over its first winter. The driveway between the coach house and Sibbald House, where Frank Sibbald had hosted garden parties, was enclosed to form part of the main dining room, and another wing, named the Bourchier Wing, was built the following year. The addition of an indoor swimming pool made The Briars truly a year-round resort.

Today, to ensure that The Briars remains in the Sibbald family, John and Barbara's sons, Hugh and Andrew, are both working for the "family firm."

THE BRIARS GOLF CLUB

Around 1920 Jack Sibbald leased part of his land "in perpetuity" for a golf course. The original nine-hole course, now known as the "front nine," was laid out by Stanley Thompson in 1922 and opened for play the following summer. A country-club house opened in August 1923, and "guests," mostly friends and neighbours of the Sibbalds, came to play golf and bridge.

The Briars Golf Club hit the headlines of the Toronto Star of July 18, 1949. The headline read: "Police nab slot machines at Jackson's Point party." The article went on to say that two York County plain-clothesmen, attending a charity function at the clubhouse on Saturday night, had waited and watched until about 10:30, when they announced their presence and seized "a slot machine and several pieces of gambling equipment." The police chief was quick to point out that it was "outsiders" who had rented the club; the club members had nothing to do with the machines, although many were in attendance at the party. Paul Higgins, a Toronto lawyer, stated that the club had been holding its annual fund-raising gala to collect money for a party to be held for children living in Georgina Township and on the Georgina Island Indian reservation. The Star went on to report that, after the raid, the party continued.

At a special meeting of the Briars Golf Club's shareholders held on August 27, 1971, it was decided to enlarge the course to eighteen holes. The "back nine," laid out by Robbie Robinson, opened in the fall of 1973.

The availability of golf, as well as the other recreational facilities of the area, brought many people who built cottages along the lakeshore and on the banks of the Black River. One of these early cottage owners was Colonel Harold Northey Gzowski, an avid golfer who taught his grandson Peter to play the game. Today, the Briars golf course is home to Peter Gzwoski's annual golf tournament for literacy.

The Briars tournament for literacy has inspired similar tournaments all across Canada, from Victoria, British Columbia, to Prince Edward Island. Jack Sibbald surely never could have imagined the effect his original nine-hole golf course would eventually have on so many Canadians.

Springwood was a popular vacation spot for many Toronto doctors and their families.

– Georgina Historical Society Postcard Collection

Just south of Jackson's Point, on the lakeshore, is Spring House, built around 1889 by Alexander Sedore at the request of Frank Sibbald. Spring House was built over a spring originating on the land side of the Lakeshore Road and emerging at the lake's edge. A large oak keg was sunk into the sand to collect the mineral water.

People were sure that because of the water's strange taste of "iron and sulphur," it had a healthful value. The spring soon became known, and everyone in the neighbourhood came to fill their jugs and bottles with the special water.

Across the road, a campground sprang up, called Springwood. Word soon spread as far as Toronto about this new campground and its healthy water and air, and Springwood was frequented over the years by many, including doctors and their families.

The Valdai Rest Home opened on June 14, 1924.
– NATIONAL SANITORIUM ASSOCIATION, REPRODUCTION BY URSULA LIANE

Glen Sibbald, built as a boarding house near Jackson's Point around 1900, was bought in 1924 by Mrs. E. L. Bonnick of Toronto and donated to the Samaritan Club to be run as a rest home for young families whose children had been afflicted with tuberculosis. The home was named the Valdai Rest Home after Mrs. Bonnick's daughter who had died of tuberculosis.

At the time, it was felt that open-air treatment, including plenty of rest and fresh air (preferably near a lake), was by far the best medicine for tuberculosis. North America's first fresh-air sanatorium was opened by Dr. Livingston Trudeau on Saranac Lake in New York State, and those that followed in Canada copied his pattern: They were built away from urban centres and provided plenty of space and good food. The patients lived in long, unheated buildings with beds lined up along one wall; the other wall was full of windows, which were opened wide, even in winter.

Sir William Gage (1849–1921), the founder of a large Canadian publishing firm, had wanted to become a doctor originally. He had been enormously affected by the fate of a childhood friend whose family had been wiped out by tuberculosis. He donated $25,000 and offered the use of his cottage in Muskoka for the creation of the Muskoka Cottage Hospital at Gravenhurst. It opened in 1897 with thirty beds. Soon the Muskoka Free Hospital was built for those who could not afford treatment. But the disease was endemic in crowded city conditions, and these two facilities did not come close to meeting the demand for treatment. William Gage next bought a farm in Weston, west of Toronto, and opened the Toronto Free Hospital for Consumptives there in 1904.

Transportation of patients to the hospitals in Muskoka proved to be increasingly difficult, so Mrs. Bonnick, a member of the Samaritan Club, set out to purchase property closer to the city. She bought Glen Sibbald at Jackson's Point for $15,000. The Samaritan Club was pleased to get Glen Sibbald, feeling that it offered many advantages: the therapeutic breezes off Lake Simcoe, good buildings, and convenience to Toronto — the Metropolitan Radial Railway cars stopped right at the gate.

By 1957 tuberculosis had almost been eliminated in North America, and the hospitals were closed. Today the West Park Hospital in Weston maintains only twenty-eight beds. Proceeds from the sale of Christmas seals, which formerly went for the treatment of tuberculosis, are now used for research and treatment of all respiratory diseases.

The Muskoka Free Hospital is now the Ontario Fire College. Glen Sibbald continued to operate until 1948; that year, over three hundred mothers and children holidayed on the shores of Lake Simcoe.

Today the house still stands in Jackson's Point, where it is used as a private residence.

Lakeshore Road in front of Glen Sibbald around 1910.

– Metropolitan Toronto Reference Library Postcard Collection

Taken around 1920, this is one of the earliest pictures of the Salvation Army camp at Jackson's Point.

– SALVATION ARMY HERITAGE CENTRE COLLECTION   3084 (D)

The Salvation Army was founded in London, England, in 1865 by William Booth. Booth, a Methodist preacher, disliked the way most Christian churches segregated the rich and the poor, so he founded his own mission to promote the "salvation of the masses." In Canada, Salvation Army corps were established in London, Toronto, Hamilton, and Chatham in 1882.

Three hundred children attended the Salvation Army's first "fresh-air" camp in August 1902 in an orchard near Oakville. Eight years later, land near Clarkson was bought for a permanent camp for underprivileged city children. In 1916 it was decided to sell the Clarkson property and purchase land on Lake Simcoe. Accordingly, the Army bought the Mossington property on Land's End. The only building, a log cabin, was demolished in 1930 and replaced by boarding house and six cottages. Later, around 1936, the adjoining Scott farm was acquired and a larger cottage built.

The Salvation Army advertised this new camp as a place "where city youngsters could get their vitamins, floods of stimulation, and hours of play in the cool glades."

Wake-up bells rang at 6:00 A.M. After breakfast and a flag-raising ceremony, the children made their own beds and did chores such as carrying water, washing dishes, and cleaning the yard. The older children were responsible for the younger ones.

Swimming classes were a highlight of each day's activities. Girls swam in the mornings, while the boys enjoyed a dip each afternoon. Boat rides were often provided by neighbours, who also treated the children to candy and ice cream.

The gates to the Salvation Army camp were built in 1926 when it was used as a Girl Guide camp.

DE LA SALLE CAMP

The De La Salle camp at Jackson's Point, sponsored by the Brothers of Christian Schools, opened in 1916. Boys from many parts of North, South, and Central America attended the camp each summer for many years after that.

In 1947 Frank Ernst and Colonel Hudson of Buffalo, who had bought war surplus equipment, donated an American LCI (Landing Craft Infantry) to the camp to be used as a recreational vehicle. After that, boys and leaders could be recognized from a distance as they cruised the lake in what looked like an old barge.

The camp was sold in 1982, and the dining hall, which had also served as a parish church and recreation centre, was moved. The LCI was converted to a cruise boat, touring Frenchman's Bay. The Town of Georgina developed the De La Salle lands and opened them as a park in 1991. De La Salle Park includes a beach, a small-boat harbour, picnic areas, playing fields, and a children's playground. The completely renovated dining hall is used by day campers as a recreation centre.

A group of boys and their leaders preparing for a cruise aboard the La Salle.

– CHRISTIAN BROTHERS ARCHIVES

The Red Barn Theatre in the early 1950s. "Canada's most unique and famous summer theatre on the shores of Lake Simcoe."

– METROPOLITAN TORONTO REFERENCE LIBRARY POSTCARD COLLECTION

Summer stock, or summer theatre, actually began in Canada in the late 1880s, but really began to spread in the late 1940s when commercial theatres began opening up in the country's resort and cottage areas. One of the first of these was the Red Barn at Jackson's Point.

The barn itself had been built in 1876 to house Holsteins on Frank Sibbald's farm. Its life as a theatre began in 1949 when actress Steffi Lock and her husband, Alfred Mulock, organized a group of actors and rented the old barn from

John Sibbald, the farm's current owner. The Mulocks invested $20,000 to turn the barn into a "straw hat" theatre similar to the Straw Hat Players Company which had been launched in Port Carling the year before. With the help of Toronto architect Harry Kohl and some students from the Ontario College of Art, the barn was renovated. A stage was built and 290 tip-up seats installed. These had been donated by Charles Bochner, president of the Canadian Theatre Chair Company and father of actor Lloyd Bochner. The seats probably had been rescued from a darkened Toronto movie house. Nothing else was altered; the barn was still a barn, only recently vacated by the livestock.

During that first summer, the company put on light comedies and sentimental dramas, opening with the play *The Voice of the Turtle*. Opening night, July 6, 1949, was reported in the Toronto *Star*: "The Barn, still looking like a barn on the outside, inside looked like the most modern theatre you could find. People and cars were turned away, and, despite a two-hour delay of the curtain rising due to a local hydro shortage, the audience left in an enthusiastic mood." The *Star* also noted that the Mulocks were looking for more apprentices. A young comedy team from Toronto auditioned and were offered jobs; John Wayne and Frank Shuster starred in the Broadway farce *Boy Meets Girl*. Others who "played the Barn" in those early days included Dinah Christie, Cecil Linder, Lloyd Bochner, Kate Reid, Toby Robins, Gordie Tapp, Walter Massey, and Hal Jackman.

During the Red Barn's first season, a close friend of the Mulock family, Harry Belafonte, is said to have staged an impromptu performance. He and Alfred Mulock christened the barn by breaking a bottle of ale on the silo.

The following year, Brian Doherty, who later founded the Shaw Festival, assumed control of the Red Barn. The Barn Stormers, an all-Canadian professional company formed by Doherty and Roy Wolvin, presented an eight-week season of musical revues. In August Barbara Hamilton played in a show called *One for the Road*, which also starred John Pratt and an American actor, Robert Herget. After the season ended, Herget returned to New York, where he appeared in a musical revue called *Razzle Dazzle*. When a young comedienne was needed, Herget immediately thought of Barbara Hamilton.

Brian Doherty stayed on at the Barn for a second season, this time trying out more traditional summer stock. He cabled actress Amelia Hall at her London, England, home: "Red Barn available for summer. Would you like to rent it?" The immediate reply was "Yes." Amelia rented the barn for $100 a week, and Doherty, in turn, shared with her his knowledge of running a theatre and of public relations.

One problem facing Amelia was where the cast and crew would live during the summer. She found a "two-storey annex" (really a back shed) at the Lake Simcoe Hotel in Jackson's Point, and obtained it for a low rent. The cast and crew could eat in the hotel's main dining room, but there was no maid service. Amelia didn't worry; as she stated, "I'll play matron and hand out clean linen every week." Others stayed at a nearby cottage, which they nicknamed the Swamp.

In 1954 the Red Barn and eight acres of land were sold to James Farrell, who invited casts and crews to continue operating a summer theatre in his barn. When Mr. Farrell died the following year, the land was sold to Max Gold, who had a summer home across the road.

The Red Barn Theatre lacked stability until 1959, when Marigold Charlesworth, Jean Roberts, and Alan Nunn took over its operations. Marigold managed to produce the barn's first profitable season, and in 1962 she took the Red Barn Production Company to Orillia before introducing a winter theatre at Toronto's Central Library.

During the winter of 1964, flames were spotted in the barn by an alert neighbour. Luckily, the barn itself was saved, and only eight seats needed replacing. One hundred seats were purchased from an old casino in Toronto for a dollar each.

Over the next few years, the Red Barn Theatre found itself facing a threat as serious as fire. Investors had found the area and began suggesting "development." In 1969

THE ANNEX

The "Annex" of Lake View House in 1940. The Lakeview property remained in the Sanders family for over 100 years.

  –THE AUTHOR'S POSTCARD COLLECTION

Max Gold sold the property to a development company. Bill Glassco took over running of the theatre in 1970, but financial difficulties and the threat of demolition hung over it. The Barn was dark during the summer of 1972 amid rumours of a planned subdivision on the site.

In February 1973 a developer offered the Barn to Georgina Township Council in lieu of land he had been asked to set aside for a park, and local residents and businessmen set out determinedly to save it. At the first meeting of the "Save the Red Barn Committee," a consortium of twelve was formed, with John Sibbald as chairman. By June it could be announced that the barn had been saved from demolition, and along with the surrounding property, it was handed over to the newly formed Lake Simcoe Arts Foundation.

The theatre opened that summer with John Dee as artistic director. Eight plays were scheduled for July and August, and clean-up crews, consisting of committee members and neighbours, spent weeks painting, picking up trash, renovating the interior of the barn, and helping build and repair props and scenery. Cattle stalls were transformed into dressing rooms. The stables served as storage places for props and scenery. Ancient bales of hay were taken out and costumes put in their place. The old bull pen is now the men's washroom and a chicken coop houses the box office.

Dark for only two seasons, Canada's oldest professional summer stock theatre was back in business. *Barefoot in the Park* opened just over a month after the go-ahead decision was made.

That "first" season of the present Red Barn was well attended — eventually. At first, volunteers, cast, and crew stood out on the Hedge Road waving people in. Hastily called-in friends and neighbours came to fill up the seats and "make it look good for the cast." But it didn't take long for word to spread, and soon the Barn was playing to capacity audiences. Many neighbours and "Friends of the Barn" volunteered their services and learned about show business and the running of a theatre. It was great fun and a great education!

The Red Barn's mascot made his theatrical debut in that 1973 season. Bartholomew the bat made his entrance appropriately enough at a press conference held just before opening night. He glided gracefully across the lobby, alighting at the feet of a startled female reporter. Bartholomew, or Bart, spent his first season flying back and forth across the stage, many times upstaging and unnerving the actors but never bothering the audience. One of his more dramatic, well-timed fly-pasts occurred during a performance of *You Know I Can't Hear You When the Water's Running*. Actor Tom Celli, portraying an old gentleman in a wheelchair, birdwatching from his front porch, raised his binoculars and shouted, "There's a red-throated, yellow-bellied sapsucker!" In zoomed Bartholomew, as if on cue! Needless to say, he completely upstaged Celli.

Later that season, Bartholomew appeared with a mate, Beatrice. One play had a scene inside a spooky old mansion, and both Bartholomew and Beatrice appeared each night during this scene, looping and rolling across the stage.

The Red Barn today continues to run productions during the months of July and August under the direction of the Lake Simcoe Arts Foundation, making it the oldest summer stock theatre in Canada, pre-dating both the Stratford (1953) and Shaw (1962) festivals.

PUBLIC TRANSPORTATION on north Yonge Street began in 1825 when Louis Bapp carried travellers from York to Holland Landing in a covered wagon or ox-cart. At Holland Landing, the passengers could board small schooners that sailed to various ports of call around Lake Simcoe. Bapp's wagons stopped for half an hour at taverns along the way, with a one-hour stop at the Newmarket Hotel. Later, Bapp inaugurated an irregular covered-wagon service from York into Georgina Township and on to Beaverton, with Thornhill and Belhaven serving as the two major rest stops on the route.

The Belhaven Hotel was often used as an overnight stop. This hotel was owned by M. Bouvain but operated for many years by Willy Culverwell. The "Culverwell Hotel" burned down in 1895, but the driving shed, with its uniquely designed doors, is still standing in the village. It housed the horses on the lower level, while upstairs a meeting hall served the community for dances, Sunday school meetings, council meetings, and auction sales.

George Playter began a wagon run in 1827 between York and Holland Landing, and the next year he introduced a regular stagecoach service on Yonge Street. In no time, it seemed, there were many stagecoaches running up and down Yonge Street on local routes and longer treks north from the Town of York. Though there were over sixty inns and taverns along the route, Yonge Street was still unsurfaced, little more than a crude wagon track, with many detours to avoid swamps and standing water.

George Playter soon found himself in competition with William Weller. Weller's stagecoaches, which could hold up to six passengers and their luggage, were drawn by four white horses, and since Weller had the contract for carrying the Royal Mail, his stages usually arrived on time.

By 1834 both William Weller and George Playter had improved their coaches. The new coach bodies were swung on springs, which gave the coaches a swaying motion. This was not as bumpy a ride, but it was very unpleasant to those with queasy stomachs. These new, improved coaches could carry up to nine passengers, with two more riding on top with the driver. Both Weller's and Playter's coaches travelled to Holland Landing, where passengers could board steamers for ports such as Orillia, Barrie, and Beaverton. Until 1853, when the railway reached Barrie, this was the only route from York north to Barrie and Orillia.

Charles Poulett Thompson of Summer Hill, near York, was connected at some time with almost every mail and stagecoach service on Yonge Street between Toronto and Lake Simcoe. Thompson had purchased William Weller's old coaches, and he ran two coaches daily on the York–Holland Landing route. His coaches left York at

One of Johnathan Thompson's stagecoaches used on the Lake Simcoe route around 1895.

– METROPOLITAN TORONTO REFERENCE LIBRARY   T13388

The Sir John Colborne *was the first steamer on Lake Simcoe.*

7:00 A.M. and 3:00 P.M., taking six hours to complete the thirty-five-mile journey to Holland Landing; the trip south to York took an hour less, being downhill all the way. Thompson entered into a partnership with Captain William Laughton, who operated boats on Lake Simcoe. This union continued until a misunderstanding destroyed the partnership in 1850. Charles Thompson then built the steamer *Morning* to run in opposition to Captain Laughton's *Beaver*. Laughton soon retaliated by establishing another stage-line on Yonge Street, and then extended his service north of Lake Simcoe with the addition of a boat called *The Gore* on Lake Huron. This rivalry continued until 1853, when Ontario's first railway, the Ontario, Simcoe & Huron, opened north to Machell's Corners (Aurora).

This rail line (commonly known as the Oats, Straw, and Hay Route) severely cut into the stagecoach business. In fact, that year the four-horse stagecoaches ceased to operate on Yonge Street south of Machell's Corners. A little later, a regular stage service was inaugurated from Newmarket north to Sutton, travelling along the Catering Road by way of Belhaven. The Catering Road (named for the Caterer, a carrier of people and provisions who travelled that road) was the first road to connect the village of Sutton with Yonge Street. Jonathan Thompson of Richmond Hill, who had been a stagecoach driver for William Weller for many years, eventually bought out Weller, and for another twenty-five years Thompson's stagecoaches travelled up and down Yonge Street between Richmond Hill and Thornhill, picking up passengers, mail, milk, and freight. But even this line was forced out of business with the opening of the radial line to Richmond Hill in 1899.

In 1816 there was only one small schooner on Lake Simcoe; just before the arrival of the railways in the 1850s, there were seven ships.

Down the Holland River from Lake Simcoe was the Old Soldiers' Landing, later known as the Lower Steamboat Landing. This was used during the War of 1812 as a site for a military storehouse. When regular navigation began on the lake after the war, the Lower Landing was used for the larger vessels and steamers. At this point, the termination of Yonge Street, the Holland River was seventy-five feet wide, its banks low and marshy and heavily wooded. This was the link that allowed a land and water route between York and the Upper Great Lakes.

In 1819 depots were established along the waterways of Upper Canada as "holding posts" for military arms and supplies en route to posts on the Upper Great Lakes. About this time, an armed schooner was built to sail Lake Simcoe to protect those posts at Holland Landing and Kempenfeldt Bay, and later the proposed capital at Roach's Point. The schooner was kept in commission by Joseph Johnson of Holland Landing. For a short time in the 1820s, Eli Beaman also owned and operated a schooner on Lake Simcoe, using it to transport settlers, their belongings and livestock to their land grants. With the exception of a few small boats, this was the way the shipping situation on the lake stood until about 1832.

Soon, however, the influx of settlers and the growth of trade and traffic dictated a need for better shipping facilities on Lake Simcoe. To meet this need, the half-pay officers who had taken up lands around the lake, chiefly on the western shores, established a stock company to buy a vessel. They called their boat the *Sir John Colborne* in honour of the lieutenant-governor of the day. The boat was built on the Holland River in 1831 and launched in 1832.

The *Colborne*, commanded by Captain Borland, was said to have been a "high pressure vessel," but she was not very speedy. Her first trip around the lake from Holland Landing to Kempenfeldt Bay took almost a week, with a whole day spent at Cook's Bay. Another day was spent near Orillia when her fuel supply needed replenishing. Because there was no landing site, the wood had to be brought from shore in small boats. Around the lake, stops were made at the cabin of every settler, as they were all stockholders in the enterprise.

However, the *Colborne* drew too much water to allow her to pass through the Narrows and into Lake Couchiching, so she was sold in 1833 to Charles Thompson, a stagecoach owner from Summer Hill, near York, who made improvements to increase her speed and put her into service in conjunction with his stagecoach line up Yonge Street. The *Colborne* was replaced by the shareholders with a speedier boat with shallower draught, the *Peter Robinson*. This steamer was named after one of her major shareholders. The others included William Robinson, William Kingdom Rains, James O. Bourchier, William Johnson, John Cummer, Thomas Mossington, Robert Johnstone, Mark Mossington, John Mills Jackson, Captain Mackenzie, the Canada Company, A. Smalley, Samuel Lount, George Playter, and William Laughton. Peterborough is named after Peter Robinson, who superintended the Irish immigration to Bathurst Township in 1823 and to Rice Lake in 1824.

The engine for the boat was purchased in Buffalo, shipped across Lake Ontario, and hauled up Yonge Street on a horse-drawn sleigh. The *Peter Robinson* was finally launched in the spring of 1833, after being dragged by men through the thick sediment at the bottom of the Holland River.

In 1837 the *Peter Robinson* was purchased by William Laughton, who began trips to Barrie and Oro each Monday and Friday, returning the following days, and Wednesday trips to Georgina and Thorah, returning the same evening. In both cases, return trips were made along the opposite shores. By 1839 the *Peter Robinson* was not large enough to handle passengers and freight, so the boat was completely overhauled, renamed the *Simcoe*, and Laughton put another boat, the seventy-foot-long *Beaver*, into service on the lake.

The *Beaver*, built at Thompsonville in 1845, sailed three times a week from Holland Landing to Barrie and Orillia, returning the next day. Like other vessels on the lake, the *Beaver* was also available for private and pleasure excursions. The *Beaver* sailed on the lake until 1855, when she was

Travellers boarding the ferry at Jackson's Point in 1909.

"laid up" at Barrie and sunk. The present Barrie train station covers her remains.

All along the lakeshore during the 1830s and 1840s, ports were established for the steamers to call at to deliver food, supplies, furniture, and farm implements. The procedure for setting up a port of call was simple: One merely built a large cedar wharf and hoisted a flag as a signal for the ship to call in. On the eastern shore were Smalley's Wharf, the government wharf at Roach's Point, Jackson's Point, Bourchier's Point, Sibbald Point, Virginia, and Port Bolster.

The next steamer on the lake appeared after Captain Laughton and Charles Thompson — who had a profitable arrangement involving Thompson's stagecoaches bringing passengers to Laughton's steamboat — had a falling-out. Thompson now built his own boat, the *Morning*, to extend his stagecoach line up Yonge Street.

The machinery and engines for the *Morning* were dragged up Yonge Street to Holland Landing on log rollers, and the completed ship was put under the command of Captain Thomas Bell, who later operated it in conjunction with the Northern Railway, which had been built as far as Bradford. (When the first train reached Bradford in 1855, James Bourchier of Jackson's Point was there to greet it and establish a route for shipping his cattle and produce to market. Bourchier also had his own little steamer, the *Sultana*, on which he sent cargoes of flour and lumber across the lake. At Barrie, a special bridge was built to facilitate the unloading of Bourchier's cargoes.) The *Morning* was sunk off Bell Ewart in 1860.

In 1855 the *J.C. Morrison*, considered the finest steamer on the lake, was launched at Bell Ewart by Captain Hugh Chisholm. Named for Justice Joseph Curran Morrison, then President of the Northern Railway, the $60,000 vessel was built for pleasure-seekers from the city. Andrew F. Hunter, in *History of Simcoe County* describes the *Morrison*

thus: "She was 150 feet in keel, fitted with upper cabins, and in every way a magnificent steamer for those days, and had a record of fifteen miles per hour, which is much faster than the majority of steamers on our lakes." The *Morrison* made daily trips from Bell Ewart to Beaverton and Orillia for only two years before she was destroyed by fire at Barrie on August 5, 1857. Nothing was saved except the cash and a few account books.

Undaunted, Captain Chisholm launched the *Emily May* at Bell Ewart in 1861. She was under the command of Captain Isaac May, who had named the boat for his daughter. In 1874 the *Emily May* passed into the hands of the Northern Railway Company, which changed her name to the *Lady of the Lakes*. She was eventually dismantled and sunk off Bell Ewart.

And finally, the *Enterprise*. Built in 1868 as a schooner called the *Couchiching*, the *Enterprise* was converted to a steamer in 1874 and plied the lake mainly as a pleasure boat. She carried picnickers and revellers around the lake until August 1903, when she sprang a leak on a return trip from Jackson's Point. The *Enterprise* barely made it to the Mulcaster Street wharf at Barrie before she sank. But the *Enterprise* lives on: She was the model for the *Mariposa Belle* in Stephen Leacock's *Sunshine Sketches of a Little Town*. Leacock described the boat as "a steamer [that] goes nowhere in particular, for the lake is landlocked and there is no navigation for the *Mariposa Belle* except to run trips on the first of July and the Queen's birthday, and to take excursions of the Knights of Pythias and the Sons of Temperance to and from local option townships."

The steamships of Lake Simcoe permanently disappeared with the coming of the railways, the radial line, and the automobile.

THE TORONTO & NIPISSING RAILWAY

Upper Canada's first railway opened in May 1853 between Toronto and Machell's Corners (Aurora). Officially called the Ontario, Simcoe & Huron Railway, built to connect those three lakes, it was soon dubbed the Oats, Straw, and Hay Route after its most common cargoes. Its next section opened to Bradford in June 1853, then to Barrie by October 11, reaching Bell Ewart on May 3, 1854. With a view to controlling all navigation on Lake Simcoe, the railway's directors purchased the steamer *Morning* and the wharves at Bradford and Orillia.

No railway line reached Jackson's Point or Sutton until 1877, when a branch of the Toronto & Nipissing, known as the Lake Simcoe Junction Railway, was built.

In 1868 applications were made to the Ontario government for the incorporation of two narrow-gauge railway companies. The first was for the Toronto, Grey & Bruce Railway, which would run north from Toronto through Caledon, Owen Sound, and on to Georgian Bay. The second was for the Toronto & Nipissing Railway Company, which envisioned a route between Toronto and Lake Nipissing, tapping into the vast lumber resources of that area. Politicians were opposed to the narrow-gauge concept, but prospects of opening up new lands for settlement far outweighed the disadvantages, and both applications were approved.

The first narrow-gauge railway, the Festiniog Railway in Wales, had been built to carry slate from quarries in 1836. This railway's gauge was only two feet, so it soon became known as the "Toy Railway." Horses pulled empty wagons up a steep hill, then the loaded wagons rolled downhill to Cardigan Bay. The Festiniog Railway converted to steam in 1863. Canada's first narrow-gauge railway was on Cape Breton Island in Nova Scotia. The Cape Breton Coal & Railway Company began operations in May 1871.

The Festiniog was unusually narrow. Most narrow-gauge railways were three and a half feet wide. This was considered much better than standard gauge, at four feet eight inches, for many reasons. Construction was thirty-five percent cheaper, and since the rolling stock was lighter, there was less wear and tear on the tracks and wheels. The railway's boxcars were so light that a man could easily push one along the tracks with one hand! And a new steam locomotive, developed in England by Robert Fairlie, showed great fuel economy.

By 1864 Fairlie locomotives were in demand around the world. So few Fairlie engines were in operation in North America, they were considered a status symbol. Between 1871 and 1872, five Fairlie locomotives were delivered to this country: three to the Cape Breton Coal Company; one to the Toronto, Grey & Bruce Railway; and the other to the Toronto & Nippissing line. This last was known as the Shedden 864/865.

The railway took delivery of the Shedden, named for John Shedden (1829–73), the company's first president, in the spring of 1873. John Shedden had worked on railways in Scotland, Pennsylvania, and Virginia before coming to Canada, where, with William Hendrie, he set up a cartage company and worked as a railway agent. As a builder on the Grand Trunk line, Shedden helped construct Toronto's Union Station and the Grand Trunk Railway's elevators on the lakeshore. Alas, Shedden met an untimely death on his own rail line on May 16, 1873. At Cannington, he tried to board a moving car and his foot slipped, causing him to fall between the car and the platform. He was crushed to death. It was felt that naming the newly arrived Fairlie engine after him would be a suitable memorial.

Perhaps not! The Shedden engine was described as

The Toronto & Nipissing Railway work crew in front of the Uxbridge car sheds around 1882. To accommodate the railway's narrow gauge a third rail was laid between the wider standard-gauge rails.

– UXBRIDGE-SCOTT MUSEUM

being "like a two-headed monster, fiery dragon, belching sparks and billows of black smoke from both its huge smokestacks. The double-header [so named because it had two fireboxes] roared through forest and farms until one day it just exploded!" This quote from Charles Cooper's *Narrow Gauge for Us* probably refers to an incident on January 31, 1874, when the engine blew up near Stouffville. Most of the crew were killed and there was extensive damage to the Stouffville station. The engine was repaired, but there was a second explosion in 1879, and two years later the Shedden engine was dismantled.

The Toronto & Nipissing Railway, operating between Toronto and Uxbridge, opened two months after the Cape Breton company. It was the first narrow-gauge railway in North America to take paying passengers. The Toronto, Grey & Bruce Railway did not open for business until the whole line was completed to Owen Sound in 1873.

After the Toronto & Nipissing line had received its charter in the spring of 1868, its directors had approached the townships through which their railway would pass and asked for financial assistance. The matter was first raised at a special meeting of the Scarborough Council held on December 14, 1868, where it was agreed that the request be granted — after a public vote. Finally, a by-law was passed sanctioning a bonus of $10,000 to be paid to the company. All along the route, nearly everyone was in favour of the railway being built. The Town of Uxbridge and the Township of Markham pledged their support, Markham even offering the company a bonus of $30,000 if they routed the line through their township.

The Toronto & Nipissing line ran over the Grand Trunk Railway's tracks from the Berkeley Street station to the Scarborough Junction station (on Eglinton Avenue near Markham Road) using a third rail laid between the wider, standard-gauge tracks. From there on, the line was laid with "forty-pound rails" imported from England. While the right-of-ways were being cleared, many trees were downed, including huge oaks. The good logs were sold to nearby lumber mills, while other wood was burned in great piles alongside the railway tracks. The workmen would roast crows on the hot rails, then eat them for their meals.

One of the contractors for the "earth work" was John Ginty and Company. Edward Wheler was given the contract for fencing and ties between Scarborough and Uxbridge. Wheler also agreed to build any necessary water tanks and engine sheds along the route.

The railway passed through fairly flat countryside; the only major bridge that needed to be built between Toronto and Uxbridge was at Unionville, over the Rouge River.

Before the railway was finally completed, the company put on short excursion trips for local residents. Boxcars with benches mounted around the outside were usually used. For several years, summer excursions were run from Uxbridge to Toronto, with people sitting on open flatcars. This run soon earned the nickname "the Watermelon Express" when it was noted that almost everyone came home with a watermelon from the city market.

The first official train of the Toronto & Nipissing Railway reached Uxbridge at 4:00 P.M. on July 12, 1871, after a six-hour trip from Toronto. It consisted of an engine, four flatcars loaded with iron, and one boxcar carrying officials, including the managing director, William Gooderham. Four months later, the line reached Coboconk.

Most along the route welcomed the railway, but others weren't so sure of the advantages. Many farmers felt that such a line would destroy their peace and lower their property values. In the line's first years, there were many accidents, most involving livestock. One such incident killed a cow on a grade approaching Stouffville. When the railway officials refused to make an adequate settlement, the cow's owner poured a few pails of lard onto the tracks, then watched in amusement as the engine tried to struggle up the hill.

By the time the Toronto & Nipissing reached Lorneville and joined the Midland Railway line, the now-strained budget could not pay for any "fancy" stations. Small sheds with shingled roofs were built at the stops. These consisted of two rooms: a small waiting room dominated by a pot-bellied stove and a baggage room where the station operator-agent could sit and conduct his business. Some stations were little more than lean-tos. These "flag-stops" were shown as no more than the letter F on route maps and timetables. Engineers slowed down when approaching these stations, always on the lookout for anyone waving a green flag or lantern. Even a handkerchief was sufficient to stop the train.

By the time service had extended as far as Coboconk, there were plans to continue the following spring, but the "panic of 1873" put an end to the project, and the railway never did reach Lake Nipissing.

In 1882 the Toronto & Nipissing Railway was acquired by the Midland Railway Company of Canada, a standard-gauge line, and the third rail was removed. The line was then leased to the Grand Trunk Railway, who took it over completely in 1893. In 1918 the Grand Trunk Railway became part of the Canadian National Railway system.

The Grand Trunk Railway work crew with engine #975 circa 1893.

– MARKHAM DISTRICT HISTORICAL MUSEUM   986.33.8

THE LAKE SIMCOE JUNCTION RAILWAY

On March 29, 1873, the Lake Simcoe Junction Railway was incorporated. It would create a branch line of the Toronto & Nipissing Railway from the Stouffville station north to Sutton and Jackson's Point. Many local businessmen and landowners, including J. R. Bourchier, served on the first board of directors. The charter gave the directors "full powers to lay track, construct piers and wharves on Lake Simcoe, purchase, charter, and navigate boats and vessels on the lake and the waters adjacent thereto." The charter also stipulated that the railway be completed within five years.

Narrow-gauge was adopted, and the Toronto & Nipissing Railway agreed to provide rolling stock and to operate the extension for a period of twenty-one years, in return for twenty-five percent of the gross receipts.

In 1875 Francis Shanly surveyed the line and was later awarded the contract to build the railroad for $290,000. The contract included a clause stating that no work be done on Sundays "except in case of an emergency." After much bickering, the line from Stouffville north to Jackson's Point opened on October 1, 1877. The railway and its opening was described by Stephen Leacock as "a part of that variegated network of little railways — of varied gauges and plans, all crooked as country roads, all afraid of a hill, and all trying to keep close to a steamer dock, each under different ownerships — which represents the short-sighted railway building of Ontario. The completion of the railway and the arrival of the first train was a great event, much ringing of bells and blowing of whistles; then the train itself arrived by the sash factory and the gristmill."

The railway company's principle objective seemed to be the short-routing of the Upper Lakes traffic across Ontario, and, with this in mind, in 1879 the company built a wharf at Jackson's Point large enough to hold four eight-wheeled freight cars. The railway also purchased the steamer *Enterprise*.

The coming of the railway helped both of Jackson's Point's major attractions: resort traffic in the summer, and ice-fishing and ice-harvesting in the winter. During the summer months, the railway added extra cars and advertised special fares for holidayers; in winter, ice from the lake was transported to the city in boxcars.

The arrival of the radial railway at the Point in 1907 provided a more convenient two-and-a-half-hour ride north from the Summer Hill station, and this, together with the advent of the motor car and refrigeration (spelling the demise of the ice industry at Jackson's Point), meant that the trains were losing business. When the Midland Railway Company opened its line to Sudbury by way of Pefferlaw, the need for a station at Jackson's Point virtually disappeared.

The Jackson's Point train station sat on the northern edge of the Lake Road at the park entrance. It consisted of one of the standard flag-stop waiting rooms, plus two additional shelters. When the railway was dismantled, all structures were moved into the park. The station itself was demolished some years later.

Train service between Sutton and Jackson's Point was discontinued on September 24, 1927, and the rails along the Park Road were lifted. Ten miles of the line between Stouffville and Zephyr had also disappeared. The balance of the line was turned over to the Northern Ontario district and kept in service "as required." Freight and passenger service to the area was eventually discontinued on May 19, 1928.

But three years later, the rail line came back to life for a short time. A spur line had been built from the Sutton station to a gravel pit on the Catering Road. When Conn

Smyth built his "hockey castle," Maple Leaf Gardens, in 1931, he brought gravel from the pit to College Street using the Lake Simcoe Railway line.

But it couldn't last and this rail line soon disappeared, like the radial railway, giving in to the automobile and improvements to the roads.

A radial car arrives at Sutton Station around 1912.

In 1883 Torontonian John Joseph Wright's (1847–1922) electric railway, which used a third rail to collect the current to propel the cars, was the highlight of the four-year-old Toronto Industrial Exhibition, forerunner of the Canadian National Exhibition. Although this short electric railway line didn't work properly, many realized its potential, and Wright was invited to return the following year. This time, the line was a success. The mile-long track was laid from Strachan Avenue to a point near the CNE's Dufferin gates, and two generators in the Machinery Hall provided power.

Those first cars carried fifty thousand passengers and, at five cents a ride, made over $2,500 for the fair. They were the way of the future. Within a few years, electric railway lines "radiated" west, north, and east of Toronto and other major centres. These radial railways became major factors in the development of commuter suburbs and dormitory towns in the years before the First World War.

By 1885 construction of the radial tracks had begun just north of Bloor Street. The line extended north in sections up Yonge Street. First, to Farnham Avenue; then to Eglinton; to Bedford Park; and on to the top of Hogg's Hollow. Five years later, in 1890, it had reached York Mills. By 1896 the line ended at Richmond Hill.

By September 1890 the first electric cars were running up and down Yonge Street at twelve miles per hour. The Yonge Street railroad provided a commuter link with North Toronto and with other communities. As well as passengers, the railway transported farmers' produce. Butter, eggs, cheese, and milk were carried into the city daily from points on the route. Early each morning, the cars stopped at many pre-arranged points to pick up cans of milk, the origin of the term "milk run." The evening trips were equally as slow, as the empty milk cans were returned to the farmers. Later, the radial cars also carried mail and newspapers.

In 1891 the Toronto Street Railway system was permitted to electrify its system to the city limits. Since their charter did not permit them to operate outside the city, another company, the Toronto & York Radial Company, was formed to take on this task. This process was completed in 1892.

Speed of the cars was now twenty miles per hour, and a new fare schedule was introduced, a rate of three cents per mile. The contract called for two trips each way per day. If the electric cars could not make the trip due to snow or any other cause, horse-drawn cars could be called back into service.

The engineers, surveyors, and other workers were preparing to lay tracks in the northern part of York County, but the farmers of the area opposed them as much as they could. The farmers had the same fears of the radial as they had of the steam trains, that property values would be lowered considerably. They also feared that the radials would bring "drifters" and "bums" who would steal the produce right out of their fields. Charles Theakston of Newmarket told the Toronto *Star*: "Farmers imagined that the radial would bring a lot of bums to steal the produce. One man stood at his fence with a gun and dared them to go through his cornfield. Another, a widow, took her team of horses out at night and drew out all the poles that had been put in during the day."

On September 6, 1985, John Joseph Wright, this time with his friend Charles van Dopoele, demonstrated a new concept on the electric railway — the trolley pole. Instead of collecting current in the third rail, a small wheel running under an overhead wire collected electricity to power the motors. This method was highly successful, and soon this means of current collection was being used around the world.

John Joseph Wright was a pioneer in electricity in Canada, having built the city's first power station, used to power streetlights on King and Yonge streets and to light up Timothy Eaton's department store. Wright also built Canada's first electric motor, which was used in a Yonge Street grocery to grind coffee.

The York farmers notwithstanding, by 1899 the radial railway had reached Newmarket with five trips a day in each direction. To help sell its service, the Metropolitan Railway established a park on the railway line. They bought two hundred acres of land surrounding Bond Lake, near Oak Ridges, where they built railway sidings and a loading platform and landscaped the grounds.

Sunday school picnics were soon being held in Ontario's "first electric park." A motor launch, the *Gypsy*, carried visitors to the various wharves around the lake. A merry-go-round and refreshment stands were also built in the park. During the 1901 season, over sixty thousand people enjoyed swimming, boating, concerts, and picnicking on the shores of Bond Lake. The next year a concert pavilion was built, described in the *Metropolitan Railway Guide* as "60 by 60 feet in size, with dressed spruce floors, always well oiled, illuminated at night by sixty incandescent lights, and here excursionists can 'trip the light fantastic' to the accompaniment of a piano supplied free by the management."

Electric power from Niagara Falls was supplemented by steam-generating stations built at Bond Lake and Keswick. These fed the new substations at Newmarket and York Mills, the latter being fed by means of Canada's first long-distance, high-voltage transmission line.

Gravel for constructing the road bed, timber for railway ties, and steel for bridges and railway tracks were transported to the construction sites on the line on railway flatcars shoved along by steam locomotives. At Richmond Hill, spe-

cial ploughs had to be brought in to clear away the huge boulders. The iron rails, each weighing over a hundred pounds, were hauled, six at a time, by horse-drawn wagons from the nearest railway station. Each section of the radial line was electrified only after it was completed.

The Lake Simcoe radial line paralleled the Yonge Street highway to a point south of Newmarket, where it swung eastward, arching around to Queensville, then west to Keswick. From Orchard Beach, the line paralleled the lake (far enough back to permit cottages to be built on the shore) to Jackson's Point.

In 1906 a station was built in Sutton on the corner of High Street and Dalton Road. Known as the Ontario Hydro building, it was used until 1931 as a waiting room for the radials. The building was purchased by Shea's Real Estate in 1972 and is now an office for Family Trust.

The community of Jackson's Point welcomed its first radial cars on June 1, 1907, when the Toronto & York arrived at the station. A year and a half later, on January 1, 1909, the line was opened to Sutton.

The railway's first trolley cars were long, built like railway coaches, and extremely heavy. They were black or dark green in colour and heated by electricity. The cars were double-ended; they could be driven from either end merely by changing the trolley pole. The motorman operated the car by turning a large crank. An air compressor and a pressure tank suspended below each car provided the pressure needed to operate the brakes. Passengers sat on slippery black leather seats whose backs could be flipped over to face the direction of travel. These cars travelled up to sixty miles per hour and swayed and dipped, giving the impression of a speedy roller-coaster ride. Passengers could enter the cars from either side or from the front or back. Long hickory poles were placed on each side of the entrance for them to grasp while mounting the cars. Each coach was staffed by a

One of the summer boarding houses at Orchard Beach on Lake Simcoe.

motorman and a conductor, both dressed in charcoal-grey uniforms with their ranks in brass letters on their caps.

North- and south-bound trains used the same tracks. Every few miles, "at strategic points," there was a siding for cars to pull into to pass each other. Each motorman was equipped with a telephone in his car to make sure the way was clear ahead.

The coaches were divided into two compartments: smoking (about one-third of the car) and non-smoking. For those who wanted a drink, a cup hung from a chain near a small tap and basin, and "emergency" toilet facilities were provided — a seat mounted above a long pipe through which one could see the ground rushing by below. When the Lake Simcoe line opened to Jackson's Point, fifteen new dark-green passenger cars were purchased. These cars were constructed for comfort and safety, with oak panelled interiors and leaded-glass windows in the doors.

Baggage cars carried groceries, mail, and milk or cream left by the farmers, as well as coal, lumber, and other supplies to merchants along Yonge Street. What convenience! The radial stopped right in front of their stores.

There were also work cars, which carried equipment and men to service the road beds, and during the winter, snow-ploughs, which attached to the fronts of the cars. The company also had a huge rotary plough. One year, when the line had been blocked for three days, the rotary plough was called into service, roaring through Thornhill with disastrous results to the store windows!

In 1920 the Toronto Railway Company agreed to sell the radial lines to the Ontario Hydro-Electric Power Commission. That year, the City of Toronto acquired the Toronto & York Radial Company and transferred the city portions of the lines to the newly formed Toronto Transportation Commission, while lines outside the city were turned over to Ontario Hydro. This new system was dubbed the Hydro-Electric Railway, Toronto and York Division.

In 1922 the death knell of the radials began to ring. The TTC introduced the motor bus and gradually their inner-city radials began to disappear. Final trips were made on the North Yonge radial line on March 15, 1930. Little ceremony was attached to the last run of the radials, on orders from City Council. The last car left the city limits at 12:35 A.M., the car returned to Toronto almost empty — to be expected at that time of the morning. A couple of ceremonial photos were taken, and the car was driven to the barns "to be disposed of." Ironically, that last car had been used over the years as a funeral car. Motor hearses were not common then, and the only radial car that could carry a coffin was one with a smoking section where the seats were so placed that the casket could be laid on the floor.

The next day, Gray Coach buses replaced the radial cars. This service lasted only four months, being replaced by the North Yonge Railway, which inaugurated radial service on the line to Richmond Hill.

On October 10, 1948, radial service was permanently discontinued on Yonge Street. The radials were replaced by diesel buses. The Toronto & York Radial Company lines were dismantled in stages. First to go was the branch line from Schomberg to Oak Ridges; next was the section between Jackson's Point and Newmarket; and, finally the rails between Richmond Hill and the city limits were torn up.

FISHING

THE FIRST REFERENCE to fishing on Lake Simcoe was made in 1615 when Samuel de Champlain described a framework of stakes used by the Huron to capture large quantities of fish in the narrows between Lakes Simcoe and Couchiching. This resulted in the French explorer's name for the lake: *Lac aux Claies*, Lake of the Stakes.

While visiting the Huron in 1624, Gabriel Sagard-Theodat, a Recollet missionary, noted that they caught a great fish called the *assihendo,* and that they set aside the biggest and fattest to boil and extract the oil, described as "sweet and nice as butter." Sagard described the fish as being as large as a codfish; historians suggest that he was referring to either the sturgeon or the whitefish.

The Huron had many legends and superstitions about hunting and fishing, for they feared that one day this great harvest would come to an end. They warned the French not to throw any fish bones onto a fire; this could harm spirits of the fish who would then advise the others in the lake to avoid being caught. On their fishing expeditions, the Huron took along a fish preacher who had the power to attract the fish into their nets. They also believed in a spirit of the nets who had once appeared in human form, complaining of having lost his wife. He warned that unless the fishermen could find him another wife, they would catch no more fish. Thus every fishing season began with a ceremony to gain the favour of the spirit. In this ceremony he was offered not one, but two Huron maidens as possible wives.

In the open waters and along the shoreline, natives used spears to catch the fish. They used two types of spears: a javelin and a three-pronged fork with a twelve-foot-long handle. During the day, the fish could be speared from a boat or the riverbank. At night, they were attracted with torches or by lighting fires on the shores.

In the spring of 1815, settler George Bond met some natives paddling a canoe along the lakeshore. They had several large salmon (lake trout) in their boat, and Bond had some liquor. He offered to trade one fish for liquor. The drink, he said, made one tribesman's eyes "begin to roll in his head," and before leaving, Bond had purchased not only the fish but the birchbark canoe and a fifteen-foot spear for the sum of $9.

Fishing gradually assumed a position of prime importance among the settlers of Upper Canada. Just before the War of 1812, hauls of a thousand or more whitefish were taken daily at almost any village on Lake Simcoe. This was fine when there were few villages, but as the population increased, so did the pressure on fish populations. And as fishing methods improved, the hauls became even greater. In the 1860s, Lake Simcoe's whitefish were so plentiful that they were sold to local farmers to fertilize their land.

An act passed in 1840 concerned itself primarily with the quality rather than the quantity of the fish being caught.

Fish inspectors were appointed, their duty being to ensure that each barrel contained two hundred pounds of fish "of the required quality."

After the Ontario Fisheries Act was passed in 1885, laws aimed at the protection of "game fish" dictated the methods by which fish could be caught; closed and open seasons; and set limits on the size and number of fish that could be taken from the lake.

Net-fishing for lake trout, whitefish, and freshwater herring, done during the spring and fall months, brought in huge harvests. In 1880 nine licenses were issued, covering over twenty-five thousand yards of gill net. The greatest net yardage on Lake Simcoe was issued the next year, when thirteen fishermen used over thirty-three thousand yards. By 1890, however, legislation disallowed net-fishing on Lake Simcoe, setting aside its waters for "natural propagation."

Commercial catches reached their peak in 1895 when almost 310,000 pounds of fish were reported, with lake trout and bass making up fifty percent of the catch. After that year, legislation began leaning towards the curtailment of commercial fishing on Lake Simcoe in favour of sport-fishing. A 1903 order-in-council prohibiting the sale of game fish spelled the demise of commercial fishing on Lake Simcoe.

Stricter laws followed, curtailing even sport-fishing on the lake. Jackson's Point was regularly patrolled by game wardens and inspectors. A report in the Newmarket *Era* in 1916 read:

One Victoria Day, a game warden came upon a youthful fisherman. To make sure the boy was not disobeying the law, the warden took his string of fish out of the water and found only catfish, perch, and suckers on the line. A few feet further downstream, he noted a large bass wriggling on a string weighed down by a stone. Naturally, the warden inquired as to what he was doing with this fish. "Well, you see," explained the boy. "He's been taking my bait all morning, so I just tied him up until I got through fishing."

ICE-FISHING

It was the region's natives who taught the settlers to spear lake trout or whitefish through holes cut in the ice with an axe, auger, or saw. These first fishermen squatted near the holes with nothing more than warm clothing to protect them from the cold winds. They sometimes wrapped themselves in animal skins, and eventually created a tent-like arrangement of skins that did double duty; it offered protection from the wind and it facilitated spotting the fish by eliminating overhead light and shadows. Later fishermen built wind screens, then portable huts. These were of light construction so that they could easily be lifted onto sleighs and hauled out onto the ice. Huts usually had floor space of about four feet by six feet and a bench ran along the length. Some were heated by small stoves.

The favourite Lake Simcoe ice-fishing grounds are the same as they have been over the centuries: along the east shore between Island Grove and Jackson's Point and Beaverton, and on the west shore between Kempenfeldt Bay and Orillia.

Today fisherman are transported to their huts by automobile, snowmobile, or "ice-scoot," a boat-like vehicle with propellers driven by overhauled aircraft engines. Most ice-fishermen catch whitefish, with daily catches of fifty to one hundred and fifty being quite common.

Ice-fishing continues to be one of Jackson's Point's major commercial enterprises and tourist attractions. In late February, the Town of Georgina hosts the Great Lake Simcoe Ice Derby, considered to be the largest of its kind in North America. Georgina rightly claims to be the "Ice-Fishing Capital of Canada."

A group of men from Toronto enjoy ice-fishing on Lake Simcoe near Jackson's Point around 1908.

— CITY OF TORONTO ARCHIVES   SC-244-5415

An advertising drawing used by the Lake Simcoe Ice Company in the 1890s.
– TORONTO BOARD OF TRADE'S TORONTO, 1893. COURTESY OF URSULA LIANE

During the winters of the late nineteenth century, Lake Simcoe was the scene of vast ice-harvesting operations. Large quantities of ice were sent to many parts of Canada and to the United States. Ice from Lake Simcoe was considered the best: first-class quality and, when samples were tested every year before harvesting began, never less than one-hundred-percent pure. Ice-cutting was done at points where the railway branches touched the lake — Jackson's Point, Barrie, and Orillia. Storage depots were also set up near rail lines in the city — one at Frenchman's Bay and another on Ellis Avenue near Grenadier Pond.

The Ice Union, comprising five large American compa-nies, had the most improved machinery for cutting and harvesting. Long slides were made so that the blocks could be run out of the water into the railway cars or into icehouses.

The Spring Water Ice Company was started in 1870 near Davenport and Avenue roads in Toronto by James Fairhead. Spring Water ice was harvested every winter from Lake Simcoe and from smaller bodies of water in and around the city, including Grenadier Pond in High Park, Bond Lake, and Lake Wilcox. It was stored in sawdust for summer delivery to butchers, hotels, and restaurants in the city. In 1894 the com-pany's name was changed to the Lake Simcoe Ice Company to capitalize on the lake's reputation for pure, clear water.

Around 1890 James Fairhead set up the Knickerbocker Ice Company on the shores of Lake Simcoe. They next year, the fierce rivalry among the many ice companies made him decide to specialize in the domestic trade and, seeing the increasing demand for Lake Simcoe ice, he set up another ice-harvesting site across the lake at Bell Ewart. This village had been named by James Bell, but Fairhead changed the spelling in his company name so the signs of his wagons would look a little classier; the new company's name was the Belle Ewart Ice Company. In 1911 Fairhead took over another ice company and began harvesting ice from Lake Wilcox. All these sites were on a rail line, allowing easy access to the markets in Toronto.

At about the same time as he set up the Knickerbocker

Ice blocks were cut by hand. One 3-foot-thick block of ice could weigh up to 150 pounds.

– ARCHIVES OF ONTARIO BOYD COLLECTION   A0160

Ice Company, Fairhead built four large icehouses, with a capacity of ten thousand tons, at Jackson's Point.

Inside the icehouses, a foot of sawdust insulation was packed between the ice and the outside walls. Railway boxcars had their doors stuffed with hay to stop the ice from thawing. Up to forty carloads of ice were moved out each night during the peak season, bound for the city markets.

Ice-harvesting operations could not begin until the ice was at least a foot thick, since it had to bear the weight of the horses, men, and equipment. If the ice surface was not particularly smooth, a field planer would break up the frozen slush after a thaw. Ice-cutting was done by men with long handsaws, followed by eight or more horse-drawn scrapers, each ten feet wide. Blocks were marked out by a channel marker with its teeth set at twenty-two or thirty-two inches. Depending on the thickness, one block of ice could weigh as much as one hundred and fifty pounds.

One row of blocks was pried loose to create a channel through which a "raft of ice" could pass. A horse and cable towed these rafts through the channels to the shorelines. After especially cold nights, the channels had to be reopened by men standing by the channel with a splitting bar, a heavy two-pronged "fork." The channels led to long conveyor belts designed to pick up the ice blocks and transport them into the icehouses or railway cars. As the cars and houses were filled, the ramps were easily moved to direct the blocks into the next depot.

The Lake Simcoe Ice Company's house at Jackson's Point consisted of eighteen rooms, each a hundred feet long, thirty feet wide, and thirty feet high. The main elevator was located in the middle of the house so that rooms on each side could be loaded simultaneously. The snagman loaded the blocks onto ten-foot wooden skids and sent them into the rooms where they were stacked, first in one direction then the other. A good crew could load up to eight freight cars or rooms at once.

Ice harvesters earned up to thirty-two cents an hour in winter and spent their summer months working on the railway. Horses were taken back to the city to pull the ice wagons.

With more than thirty horse-drawn ice wagons on Toronto's streets, James Fairhead soon became known as "The Ice King." At one time, the Lake Simcoe Ice Company had two hundred and twenty-five horses and twenty-five wagons delivering ice to the city and suburbs. Each morning, before setting out on their routes, the drivers had to groom their horses and wash down their wagons. The Lake Simcoe Ice Company also sold ice tools, such as planers and scrapers.

In 1914 the Lake Simcoe Ice Company began to make plans to manufacture rather than simply harvest the ice. James Fairhead had noted the many disadvantages of his company's methods of harvesting and storing the ice blocks. It was difficult to keep the blocks a standard size to fit into the iceboxes of the day. The sawdust in which the ice blocks were stored had to be washed or scraped away. There were delays on the railroad lines to deal with, and if there should happen to be a mild winter, as there had been in 1906, for instance, there could be real difficulties in the ice business.

Toronto's first ice-making plant was built in 1915 on Dupont Street. Over the next fifteen years, the Lake Simcoe Ice Company built three more ice-making plants, and the storage depots were gradually dismantled. In 1929 the company was enlarged to also market coal oil, fuel, and to install heating and refrigeration equipment.

With the coming of machines for making ice, the harvesting operations on Lakes Wilcox and Simcoe were closed down. Today the Lake Simcoe Ice Company is a thriving independent company specializing in ice-making and cold-storage facilities.

In 1967 Bonnie Boats built these modern boat slips but retained the "Grew" sign.

— JEANNE HOPKINS

In 1883 Arthur Grew began making canoes, rowboats, and sailboats at Jackson's Point. The Grew family had bought land on Lake Simcoe, hoping its fresh, clear air would help relieve young Arthur's asthma. Just up the road, beside the Lake Simcoe Hotel, Arthur Grew built a stone house; the front door is said to contain planks from the steamer *Enterprise*, which sank off a wharf near Barrie in 1903.

In the late 1930s Grew Boats had over a hundred craft on the lake, when the building of small boats developed almost overnight into a vast wartime activity. During the Second World War, the Fairmile Association was formed to co-ordinate the activities of several firms, including Grew Boats, at that time of Penetanguishene and Jackson's Point, in producing the Fairmile, a new wartime craft.

The Fairmile B, a one-hundred-and-twelve-foot launch, was built of mahogany, teak, and oak and powered by two gasoline engines. These boats carried depth charges, gun units, and the latest scientific sounding and listening devices to detect any submerged submarines. After the first Fairmile was launched on July 24, 1941, Jackson's Point became a training ground for sailors who would see action overseas.

After the war ended, the company designed and built a new twenty-three-foot boat that was dubbed the "Bonnie Boat." Clarence Kemp had assumed ownership of the company, and he later sold the Grew trademark and boat plans to Gidley Boats in Penetanguishene. The little company that remained in Jackson's Point took the name Bonnie Boats.

In 1952 Stan and Bill Sellers bought Bonnie Boats and built a canal and thirty new boat slips. A new boathouse was built in 1967, and the original Grew workshop was moved offshore, where it now serves as a storage shed.

In 1986 the Gidley Company was recognized as the largest manufacturer of powerboats in Canada, with over twenty-five hundred boats being produced. Two years later, the company was forced to close down when people stopped buying pleasure craft. Two of Gidley's former employees started their own company, Roamer Boatworks, at Penetanguishene, but this firm could not survive. Grew Canada's plant came back to life in the spring of 1992, this time concentrating on making thirteen- to twenty-three-foot boats to sell for under $10,000. Bonnie Boats at Jackson's Point is still in operation.

By the war's end, almost all the Fairmiles had disappeared or were scrapped. One that survived is said to be still plying the waters of Lake Muskoka as a pleasure craft.

The D. MacDonalds's cottages at Jackson's Point in 1900.

– Archives of Ontario Frank Smily Papers. *Canadian Summer Resort Guide 1900* pamph. 1900, no. 75

JACKSON'S POINT'S other major industry, tourism and recreation, came with the railways. When the Lake Simcoe Junction line reached the Point and the southwestern shore of Lake Simcoe in 1877, boarding houses, campgrounds, hotels, and private cottages opened up along the now accessible lakefront playground, leading to its development as "Ontario's first cottage country."

Even before the railway reached Jackson's Point, however, the area had been the scene of many excursion parties, Sunday school picnics, and other outings, with holidayers crossing the lake on chartered steamers. When the Toronto & York radial line arrived in 1907, the area became a favourite summer destination for a whole generation of Torontonians.

Jackson's Point Park officially opened on June 29, 1885. The fourteen-acre park, according to the Newmarket *Era,* was "beautifully situated, with a commanding view of the lake and the surrounding shores. In the immediate vicinity are Snake, Fox, and Georgina Islands. The beach is formed mostly of sand and pebbles and affords every facility for bathing and boating purposes. The shore is well lined with birch, maple, elm, oak, and ash, and everywhere are delightful shady retreats, most advantageously suited for picnicking and camping."

Plans were next made to erect a hotel on the lake.

F. G. Tremayne, secretary and treasurer of the Jackson's Point Hotel Company, and D. W. MacDonald stated that they intended to "fit up suitable grounds for baseball, cricket, and lacrosse." Cricket and lacrosse matches were both popular at the time, and various towns on the lake had teams. After a cricket team from Orillia was victorious in one match at Jackson's Point, they were forced to delay their return home because the captain of the *Enterprise* refused to sail in the heavy winds and waves. At 3:00 A.M., after calling all passengers aboard with the boat whistle, the *Enterprise* set sail, reaching Orillia three hours later. Even at that hour, most of the townspeople were out to greet the boys, having been awakened by the ringing of the firebell.

It didn't take long before Toronto business interests saw the potential in developing a resort hotel at Jackson's Point, and in 1887 a conglomerate from the Grand Trunk Railway Company met to discuss such a project. George Stephen (later Lord Mountstephen) was president of the Grand Trunk Railway Company at that time, and his company had opened its first hotel, the Hotel Vancouver, that year. Mr. Stephen felt that Jackson's Point was "one of the finest places in America for a summer resort."

To further sell interest in the hotel, an excursion was arranged by the railway company. Many members of the

Toronto Board of Trade and other wealthy Torontonians were invited. At Jackson's Point, the train was met by directors of the hotel company, and the Newmarket *Era* said, "A very acceptable dinner was laid out on long tables in a beautiful grove." After a sail on the steamer *Orillia*, the party returned to the city. The hotel never materialized.

Jackson's Point had by this time also become a popular summer playground for residents of other points on the railway line. Lake View House was owned by Stouffville lumber dealer William B. Sanders. Sanders began to subdivide his land at the Point and sell lots to his friends. Lumber for the cottages was cut from the Lake View property or shipped by train from Sanders's yards in Stouffville. In 1885 Sanders's hotel had one hundred and twenty rooms; five years later, there were thirty more.

Those five years also saw a boom in the number of hotels in the area. Simkincoe House, Glen Sibbald, and Jackson Villa were among those added to the list, which in 1885 already had included the Jackson's Point Hotel, Rotherwood, and Albert Mossington's Plumstead.

To realize the popularity of Jackson's Point in the late 1800s, we can read newspaper accounts, such as this one from 1888, of Dominion Day celebrations at the Point.

Lodge 2, Sons of Canada, from Toronto, celebrated Dominion Day by an excursion to Jackson's Point. Two large train loads, the first under the charge of Conductor Charlie Mitchell, the other by Dan McMillan, containing about 1,000 people, reached the Jackson's Point Park at 11:00 A.M. having made the run from Toronto in about two hours and a half. Here they immediately proceeded to enjoy themselves — some boating and fishing, others tripping the light fantastic on the fine dancing platform lately erected, to the strains of the first-class Quadrille Band. A large number took advantage of the hourly trips run by the steamer Kendrick

under the command of Captain W. W. Ramsay to Georgina Island; others explored the shady nooks and lovely walks for which Jackson's Point is noted. Buses were constantly running to the cricket grounds where base ball was played throughout the day.

In later years the same newspaper, the Toronto *Star*, reported:

It is the custom on Dominion Day for all who live within a reasonable distance to come to Jackson's Point and have a big picnic. Some come on the electric car, some on the morning train, while those who live near come in their buggies. The town line was one long string of vehicles and buggies.

Jackson's Point and the lake shore is fast gaining in popularity and judging from the numbers of doctors who are rusticating there, must be thought to be very healthy. The families of Dr. Semple and MacDonald are at the cottages on Jackson's Point and express themselves as highly pleased with the arrangements made by the hotel company for their comfort and with the railway facilities of reaching it, Dr. F. Black and family are at the Old Parsonage near the lakeshore church in company with Mr. H. G. Park, Dr. Forest of Mount Albert, with his brother Dr. Forest of Bradford, and their families are camped in Dr. Sibbald's woods at 'The Briars'.

By 1889 the park at Jackson's Point included a large dining hall where meals could be bought at any hour for twenty-five cents. Boats for hire, refreshment booths, swings, and large dance platforms were among the many attractions at the Point. Many Toronto families spent the entire summer there, renting rooms in the various hotels and boarding houses on the lakeshore.

Lake Simcoe, especially off Jackson's Point, was the scene of much recreational boating. In the late 1890s, dinghy races were held regularly on Saturday mornings,

The Lake View House at Jackson's Point around 1910.

– Metropolitan Toronto Reference Library Postcard Collection

The crowded buggy parking lot at Jackson's Point during the Lennox picnic of 1911.

with many of the local yacht clubs competing for prizes. Annual regattas were sponsored in August by the Lake Simcoe Association from 1907 on, and included teams from Eastbourne, Orchard Beach, Jackson's Point, Roche's Point, and De Grassi Point. Swimming, skiffing, single-, double-, and mixed-canoe (four in a canoe) sailing, and war canoe races were all part of the day's fun. The fourth annual regatta, in 1911, was reported in the Newmarket *Era* as "a great success with about 2,000 attending. Music was furnished by a piper from the 48th Highlanders. A dance and distribution of prizes followed the day's activities."

It was around this time that motor launches began to appear on the lake. They were such a novelty that they were reported on the social pages. "Mr. Kemp's new launch, appropriately named *Rownamore* forms a splendid addition to the Lake Simcoe fleet of pleasure craft. She was tried out a few times last week and can easily make a speed of 12 miles per hour," reported the Toronto *Star* in 1906. The following year, the *Star* announced the arrival of another motor launch and brought to light a rather strange appetite of the lake's fish population.

Mr. J. F. Brown of Toronto has placed a new boat in commission. It is a gasoline boat, 26 feet long, with a 14-horse power engine. It went over to the island for a fish last week and succeeded in landing a few of the good ones, but in the excitement, the fish got at his gasoline and drank it to the dregs, and when they started for home, he found to his dismay that the juice had disappeared, but the island was only five miles away and he soon had his tank refilled.

Jackson's Point and area was also the scene of Thomas Herbert Lennox's yearly "rendezvous" or political picnic. After serving on Aurora Town Council for three years, Lennox was elected to the Legislative Assembly for the riding of North York. In 1925 he tried his hand at federal politics and was elected to the House of Commons, representing York North until his death in 1934.

Herb Lennox had a cottage at Mossington's Park, and from 1905 on he threw a lavish annual celebration with guests arriving by boat, horse and buggy, and on horseback.

At the Lennox picnic held in July 1910, it was estimated that over four thousand were brought by the Metropolitan Railway, and that boats from Bradford and Barrie brought over another thousand, while over a thousand more drove to the gates from the surroundings areas. "The rush for cars about five o'clock was tremendous and hundreds had to wait for hours before they could get into a car. For a couple of hours, cars left every fifteen minutes. It was midnight before all the crowd was picked up," reported the Newmarket *Era*.

The next year's picnic drew over fifteen thousand, and became the "Annual Conservative Picnic for North York." That year, Lennox had hired a special Grand Trunk Railway car to carry his supporters from Toronto. In keeping with "political tradition," speeches by Conservative members of the provincial and federal parliaments were allowed — but kept to five minutes each.

In 1915, in a spirit of wartime patriotism, the picnic became non-political and only purely patriotic speeches were allowed. The proceeds of this picnic were donated to the Red Cross. In 1916 upwards of eight hundred motors helped to relieve the railway traffic. This picnic, with proceeds going to the Red Cross and the IODE, included a parade and automobile procession from Sutton to Jackson's Point, led by fourteen brass bands. Prizes were awarded for the three best-decorated cars. The winner, James Forrest of the Toronto Railway Company, had decorated his car as a miniature warship. At the Point, there were all kinds of sports, amusements, and contests: baby shows, midway rides, a tug of war, and a huge fireworks display completed the day.

By this time the Lennox picnic had become the largest annual picnic in the world, and each year it grew larger. The biggest — and last — was held on August 7, 1933, when over twenty-five thousand jammed the picnic grounds at Jackson's Point. Lennox's death the next year brought an end to the picnics.

Jackson's Point, once the main recreation and cottage country of Ontario, fell out of favour somewhat when Highways 11 and 48 opened up the Muskoka and Haliburton regions, and the family automobile became more common. Trains stopped running to the Point in 1928, and the radial cars made their last runs twenty years later, but today Jackson's Point remains a popular summer and winter resort community.

The Mossington Park Dance Hall and Pavilion in 1990 — a relic of the past.

– ROBERT HOPKINS

Main Street, Jackson's Point, in the early 1940s.

    – Tom MacDonald Postcard Collection, courtesy of Ursula Laine

BIBLIOGRAPHY

Barry, James, P. *Georgian Bay: The Sixth Great Lake* (Toronto: Clarke Irwin, 1968)

Berchem, F. R. *Yonge Street Story 1793–1860* (Toronto: McGraw-Hill Ryerson, 1977)

Bonnycastle, Richard S. *Canadas in 1841* (New York: Johnson Reprint, 1968)

Byers, Mary; Kennedy, Jan; and McBurney, Margaret. *Rural Roots* (Toronto: University of Toronto Press, 1976)

Cameron, Donald. *Faces of Leacock: An Appreciation* (Toronto: Ryerson Press, 1967)

Cooper, Charles. *Narrow Gauge for Us: The Story of the Toronto and Nipissing Railway* (Erin, Ont.: Boston Mills Press, 1982)

Curry, Ralph. *Stephen Leacock: Humorist and Humanist* (Garden City, N.J.: Doubleday, 1959)

De la Roche, Mazo. *Ringing the Changes* (Toronto: Macmillan, 1957)

Dictionary of Canadian Biography (Toronto: University of Toronto Press, 1966)

Due, John Fitzgerland. *Intercity Electric Railway Industry in Canada* (Toronto: University of Toronto Press, 1966)

Early Canadian Life (1978)

Eildon Hall: Sibbald Memorial Museum, Sibbald Point Provincial Park (Toronto: Ontario Dept. of Lands and Forests, 1965)

Guillet, Edwin C. *Pioneer Life in the County of York* (Toronto: Hess-Trade Typesetting Co., 1946)

Guillet, Edwin C. *Pioneer Travel in Upper Canada* (Toronto: University of Toronto Press, 1966)

Hall, Amelia. *Life Before Stratford* (Toronto: Dundurn Press, 1989)

Hambleton, Ronald. *Mazo De la Roche of Jalna* (New York: Hawthorn Books, 1966)

Hambleton, Ronald. *Secret of Jalna* (Don Mills, Ont.: Paperjacks, 1972)

Hett, Francis Paget. *Georgina: A Type Study of Early Settlement and Church Building in Upper Canada* (Sutton West, Ont.: Paget Press, 1978)

Hett, Francis Paget (ed.). *Memoirs of Susan Sibbald 1783–1812* (London: John Lane, The Bodley Head, 1926)

Hunter, Andrew F. *History of Simcoe County* (Barrie, Ont.: County Council, 1909)

Ice Industry at Bell Ewart (Innisfil Historical Society, 1982)

Jameson, Anna Brownell. *Winter Studies and Summer Rambles in Canada* (Toronto: Thomas Nelson, 1943)

Kimball, Elizabeth. *The Man in the Panama Hat* (Toronto: McClelland and Stewart, 1970)

Lake Simcoe *Advocate*

Lake Simcoe and Its Environs (Barrie, Ont.: Barrie *Examiner*, 1893)

Lavallée, Omer. *Narrow Gauge Railways of Canada* (Montreal: Railfare Books, 1972)

Leacock, Stephen. *The Boy I Left Behind Me* (Garden City, N.J.: Doubleday, 1946)

Leacock, Stephen. *Sunshine Sketches of a Little Town* (Toronto: McClelland and Stewart, 1970)

Legate, David M. *Stephen Leacock: A Biography* (Toronto: Doubleday Canada, 1970)

MacCrimmon, Hugh R. and Skobe, Elmars. *The Fisheries of Lake Simcoe* (Toronto: Dept. of Lands and Forests, 1970)

More Than Words Can Say: Personal Perspectives on Literacy (Toronto: McClelland and Stewart, 1990)

Munro, Mary. *Versus* (Sutton, Ont.: Sutton Printers, 1952)

Newmarket *Era*

Oxford Companion to Canadian Theatre (Toronto: Oxford University Press, 1989)

Robertson, John Ross. *Robertson's Landmarks of Toronto* (Toronto: J. Ross Robertson, 1896)

Scott, James. *Settlement of Huron County* (Toronto: Ryerson Press, 1966)

Sibbald, E. *Notes on Georgina* (Women's Canadian Historical Society Transactions, no. 16, 1916–17)

Sibbald Point Provincial Park (Toronto: Ontario Dept. of Lands and Forests, 1971)

Smith, William H. *Smith's Canadian Gazetteer* (Toronto: H. & W. Rowsell, 1846)

Trewhella, Ethel Willson. *History of the Town of Newmarket* (Newmarket, Ont.: 1967)

Toronto *Daily Star*

Toronto *Telegram*

Trout, J.M. & Edw. *The Railways of Canada for 1870–1* (Toronto: Monetary Times, 1871)

Weaver, Emily. *Counties of Ontario* (Toronto: Bell & Cockburn, 1913)

York Pioneer and Historical Society. *York Pioneer*

Aitken, Alexander	10
Baldwin, Robert	11
Bapp, Louis	45
Barn Stormers, The	42
Bartholomew the Bat	42
Barwick, John	19
Beaman, Eli	48
Beaver	47, 49
Belafonte, Harry	42
Belhaven Hotel	45
Bell, Captain Thomas	50
Bell Ewart	50, 51, 65
Bell, James	65
Belle Ewart Ice Company	65
Black River	**1**, 11, 15, 16, **17**, 18, 19, 34
Bochner, Charles	41
Bochner, Lloyd	41, 42
Bonaparte, Napoleon	32
Bond, George	61
Bond Lake	58, 64
Bonnick, Mrs. E. L.	36
Bonnie Boats	**67**
Borland, Captain	48
Bourchier, Eustace Fane	14
Bourchier, James O'Brien	11, 14, 15, 17, 48, 50
Bourchier, Captain William	11, 13, 14, 15, 17, 25, 32
Bourchier's Mills	15, 18
Bouvain, M.	45
Briars, The. *See* Briars Resort	
Briars Golf Club	30, **31**, 34
Briars Resort	29, **31**, 32, **33**, 34, 70
Brûlé, Étienne	9
Canadian National Railways	16, 54
Carrying Place Trail	10
Catering Road	47, 55
Champlain, Samuel de	9, 61
Chapman, Alfred	27
Charlesworth, Marigold	42
Chisholm, Captain	50
Chisholm, Captain Hugh J.	50
Clement, Caroline	29
Colborne, Sir John	20, 22, 25
Comer, Elizabeth Georgina	17
Comer, John	9, 17, 18, 25
Comer, Margaret	17
Couchiching, Lake	9, 30, 48
Culverwell Hotel	45
Culverwell, Willy	45
Dee, John	44
De la Hontan, Baron Louis-Armand	9, 10
De la Roche, Mazo	27, 29
De la Roche, Rene	29
De La Salle Camp	**40**
Doherty, Brian	42
Doubleday family	20
East India Company	19, 32
Egypt (Ont.)	11, 15, 28, 29-30
Eildon Hall	19, 22, 23, 26, 27, 32
Emily May	50
Enterprise	50, 55, 67, 69
Everest, Sir George,	26
Everest, George John	26, 27
Fairhead, James	64-66
Fairlie, Robert Francis	51
Fairmile Association	67
Family Compact	12, 16

Farrell, James	42	Jackson's Point Hotel	69, 70
Festiniog Railway	51	Jackson's Point Park	69, 70
First World War	57	*J.C. Morrison*	50
Gage, Sir William	36	Johnson, Captain William	16, 48
George III	11, 17, 22	Johnstone, Robert	16
Georgina Island	23, 34, 69, 70	Kemp, Clarence	67, 73
Georgina Township	7, 9, 11, 13-19, 34, 44, 45	Kempenfeldt Bay	48, 62
		Kendrick	70
Gibson, John	26, 27	Knickerbocker Ice Company	65
Gidley Company	67	*Lady of the Lakes*	50
Glassco, Bill	44	Lake Simcoe Arts Foundation	44
Glen Sibbald	36, 70	Lake Simcoe Hotel	42, 67
Gold, Max	42, 44	Lake Simcoe Ice Company	**64**, 66
Gooderham, William	53	Lake Simcoe Ice Derby	62
Gore, Francis	13	Lake Simcoe Junction Railway	51, 55, 69
Gore, The	47	Lake View House	43, 70, **71**
Grand Trunk Railway	51, 53, **54**, 69, 73	Land's End	18, 38
Grew, Arthur	67	Laughton, Captain William	47, 48, 49, 50
Grew Boats	67	Leacock, Agnes Emma Butler	**28**, 29, 30
Gwillim, Thomas	10	Leacock, Stephen Butler	27, **28**, 29, 30, 50, 55
Gzowski, Harold Northey	34	Leacock, Walter Peter	29
Gzowski, Peter	34	Lee, Eliza	19, 22
Hall, Amelia	42	Lee, Mary Ready	19,
Hamilton, Barbara	42	Lee, Simon	19, 23
Hedge Road	32, 44	Lennox, Thomas Herbert (Herb)	72, 73, 74
Henry, Alexander	9	Lloyd, Kathleen Sibbald	30
Holland Landing	8, 10, 11, 18, 22, 23, 45, 47-50	Lock, Steffi	41
		Lount, Samuel	48
Holland River	10, 48	Lower Steamboat Landing	48
Holland, Samuel	10	Lyall, Jean	15
Home District	10, 13, 16	MacDonald, D. W.	68, 69
Howard, Charles Henry	11	Machell's Corners	47, 51
Humber-Holland Trail	**8**, 10	Mackenzie, Captain	48
Indian House	23	Mackenzie, William Lyon	16
Jackson, Amelia	14	Manor House, The	32
Jackson, John Mills	**12**, 13, 25, 48	Manor (Sutton)	15
Jackson Villa	70	Maple Leaf Gardens	56

Mariposa Belle	50
May, Captain Isaac	50
Mein, Betsy Isabella	22
Mein family	22
Mein, Thomas	22
Metheral, John	23
Metropolitan Radial Railway	36, 57
Metropolitan Street Railway Company	57
Midland Railway Company	54, 55
Mitchell, Charlie	70
Morning	47, 50, 51
Morrison, J.C.	50
Morrison, Joseph Curran	50
Mossington, Albert Edward	18, 19, 70
Mossington bridge	19
Mossington family	16, 17, 18, 19, 25, 38
Mossington Mill	**17**, 18, 19
Mossington, Moses	19
Mossington, Thomas (1780–1864)	17, 18, 19, 25, 26, 48
Mossington, Thomas (1817–1896)	18, 19
Mulock, Alfred	41, 42
Muskoka Cottage Hospital	36
Northern Railway	50
Newton Brook	12, 13
Nunn, Alan	42
Oak Ridge	9
Old Soldiers' Landing	10, 27, 48
Oldcastle	16
Ontario County	11
Ontario Hydro	58, 60
Ontario, Simcoe & Huron Railway	47, 51
Orchard Beach	58, **59**, 73
Orillia	70
Park, Harry	30
Park, Samuel	26
Pefferlaw	11, 16, 55
Penetanguishene	10, 67
Penetanguishene	20
Penn Range	20, 22, 23
Peregrine, John	18
Peter Robinson	48, 49
Pine Fort	10
Playter, George	45, 48
Plumstead	18, 19, 70
Preston, Laura	14
Queen's Rangers	10
Radial Railway	47, 56, 57, 58
Rains, William Kingdom	11, 20-22, 48
Rebellion of 1837–38	15, 16, 18
Red Barn Theatre	32, **41, 42, 44**
Richmond Hill	46, 47, 57, 58, 60
Ritchie, William	26, 27
Roach, James	11
Roach's Point	11, 15, 48
Roamer Boatworks	67
Roberts, Jean	42
Robinson, Peter	48
Robinson, William	48
Roche family	27, 29
Rotherwood	17, 23, 70
Rownamore	73
Sagard-Theodat, Gabriel	61
St. George's Church	**6**, 17-19, 23, **24, 25**, 26, 32
St. George's Cemetery	27, 29, 30
Salvation Army Camp	**38, 39**
Samaritan Club	**36**
Sanders, William B.	43, 70
Second World War	26, 29, 67
Sedore family	35
Sellers, Bill	67
Sellers, Stan	67
Shanly, Francis	55

Shedden, John — 51
Shuster, Frank — 42
Sibbald, Anne — 26
Sibbald, Archibald — 22
Sibbald, Charles — 22
Sibbald, Elizabeth Kemp — 33
Sibbald family — 22, 23, 25, 30, 34
Sibbald, Francis Clunie — 22, 32, 35, 41
Sibbald, Georgina — 26
Sibbald House — **21**, 34
Sibbald, Hugh — 23
Sibbald, John — 18, 30
Sibbald, John Drinkwater (1845–1923) — 33
Sibbald, John Drinkwater (1891–1960) — 30, 34
Sibbald, John Drinkwater (1940–) — 29, 30, 34, 41, 44
Sibbald, Minnie — 19
Sibbald, Ogilvie — 22
Sibbald Point Provincial Park — 19, 23, 26
Sibbald, Susan — 6, 20, 22, 25
Sibbald, Thomas — 22, 26, 27
Sibbald, William (1771–1835) — 22, 26
Sibbald, William (1814–82) — 19, 30
Simcoe — 18, 49
Simcoe family — 6, 10, 26
Simcoe, Elizabeth — 10, 26
Simcoe, John Graves — 9, 10
Simcoe, Lake — 9, 10-11, 14, 16-18, 22, 23, 29, 30, 36, 38, 45-48, 50, 51, 55, 61, 62, 64, 65, 67, 70
Simkincoe House — 70
Sir John Colborne — **47**, 48
Smalley, A. — 48
Smalley's Wharf — 50
Smith, W. I. D. — 27

Smyth, Conn — 56
Sowby, Cedric — 27
Spring Water Ice Company — 64
Spring House — 35
Springwood — **35**
Steamboat Landing — 10
Stupart, Captain Robert Douglas — 19
Sutton West — 11, 14, 15
Sultana — 50
Thompson, Charles Poulett — 21, 45, 47, 48, 50
Thompson, Clifford — 22
Thompson, Jonathan — 46, 47
Thorpe, Robert — 11, 13
Toronto & Nipissing Railway — 51, **52**, 53-55
Toronto & York Radial Railway — 57, 58, 60, 69
Toronto, Grey & Bruce Railway — 51, 53
Toronto Transportation Commission — 60
Troop, Marjorie Temple — 33
Upper Canada — 10-13, 15-20, 22, 27, 48, 51, 61
Valdai Rest Home — **36**
War of 1812 — 10, 11, 48, 61
Wayne, Johnny — 42
Weller, William — 45, 47
Willcocks, Joseph — 12, 13
Wright, John Joseph — 57, 58
Wyatt, Charles Burton — 12, 13
Yonge Street — 10, 11, 13, 19, 23, 29, 45, 47, 48, 50, 57, 58, 60
York (Toronto) — 10-13, 16, 18, 45, 47, 48, 58
York County — 9, 11, 16, 23, 34